ICSA Study Text

Certificate in Offshore Finance and
Administration
Offshore Business Environment

ICSA Study Text

Certificate in Offshore Finance
and Administration

Offshore
Business
Environment

Carla Channing

icsa.
Publishing

First published 2012
Published by ICSA Information & Training Ltd
16 Park Crescent
London W1B 1AH

Typeset by Paul Barrett Book Production, Cambridge
Printed and bound by Marston Digital, Didcot, Oxon

British Cataloguing in Publication Data
A catalogue record for this book is available from the British Library.

ISBN 978 186072 476 3

Contents

How to use this study text

ICSA study texts, developed to support ICSA's Certificate in Offshore Finance and Administration (COFA), follow a standard format and include a range of navigational, self-testing and illustrative features to help you get the most out of the support materials.

Each text is divided into three main sections:

◆ introductory material
◆ the text itself
◆ additional reference information.

The sections below show you how to find your way around the text and make the most of its features.

Introductory material

The introductory section of each text includes a full contents list and the module syllabus which reiterates the module aims, learning outcomes and syllabus content for the module in question.

Where relevant, the introductory section will also include a list of acronyms and abbreviations or a list of legal cases for reference.

The text itself

Each **part** opens with a list of the chapters to follow, an overview of what will be covered and learning outcomes for the part.

Every **chapter** opens with a list of the topics covered and an introduction specific to that chapter. Chapters are structured to allow students to break the content down into manageable sections for study. Each chapter ends with a summary of key content to reinforce understanding.

Features

The text is enhanced by a range of illustrative and self-testing features to assist understanding and to help you prepare for the examination. Each feature is presented in a standard format, so that you will become familiar with how to use them in your study.

These features are identified by a series of icons as shown below.

The texts also include tables, figures and other illustrations as relevant.

Reference material

The text ends with a range of additional guidance and reference material, including a glossary of key terms, a directory of web resources and a comprehensive index.

Stop and think

Test yourself

Worked examples

Making it work

Case law

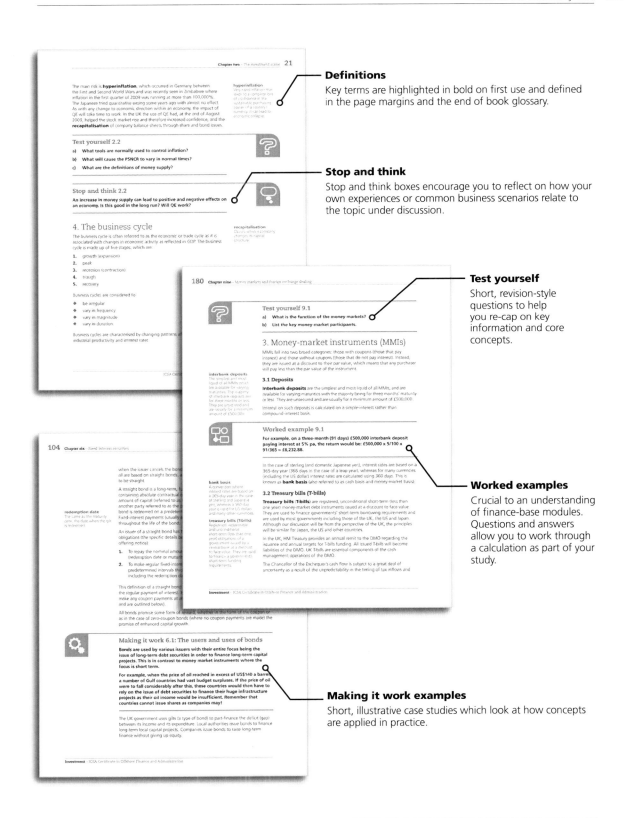

Definitions

Key terms are highlighted in bold on first use and defined in the page margins and the end of book glossary.

Stop and think

Stop and think boxes encourage you to reflect on how your own experiences or common business scenarios relate to the topic under discussion.

Test yourself

Short, revision-style questions to help you re-cap on key information and core concepts.

Worked examples

Crucial to an understanding of finance-base modules. Questions and answers allow you to work through a calculation as part of your study.

Making it work examples

Short, illustrative case studies which look at how concepts are applied in practice.

The Offshore Business Environment syllabus

Aims

This module provides an introduction to fundamental topics and issues in the offshore-services industry. Subjects covered include the types of products and services offered, the regulation and supervision of offshore financial-services providers, and anti-money-laundering regulations.

Learning outcomes

On successful completion of this module, candidates will be able to:

◆ describe typical features of offshore centres;

◆ demonstrate an understanding of key aspects of English law;

◆ outline taxation concepts;

◆ describe the principles of foreign exchange and offshore banking;

◆ explain the types of products and services typically available from an offshore-services provider;

◆ explain the significance of the regulation and supervision of offshore business, including the role of international bodies which have an effect on offshore business;

◆ demonstrate understanding of UK insider-dealing and market-abuse legislation, and the implications for organisations and individuals found in breach; and

◆ demonstrate understanding of money laundering and the issues for offshore centres in this respect, including anti-money-laundering (AML) legislation and processes, and the implications for organisations and individuals found in breach.

Syllabus

1. Offshore centres
   Development and features of offshore centres
   'Onshore offshore centres'
   Choosing an offshore centre and a services provider

2. The legal environment
The importance of English law in offshore business
Legislation, interpretation, and case law
Contract law

3. Taxation
Different taxes and their implications: direct taxation versus indirect
taxation
Residence, domicile, and tax implications
Taxation of companies, partnerships, foundations, and trusts
Transfer pricing

4. Banking
Accounts and payments
Foreign exchange
Forward-exchange contracts
Offshore-banking services

5. Offshore services
Introduction to the financial-services sector
Trusts and companies: uses and administration
Services, insurance, and legal services
Tax compliance and tax planning
Investment-management services
Retail Distribution Review (RDR)

6. Regulation and supervision of the offshore services sector
The need for and development of regulation
Regulatory codes
Money laundering, know your customer (KYC), client due diligence (CDD),
market abuse and data protection
The role and powers of international bodies

7. Insider dealing
What insider dealing is and who is involved
Penalties for insider dealing
Preventing insider dealing

8. Money laundering
Money laundering and why it is considered harmful
Anti-money-laundering (AML) and combatting the financing of terrorism
(CFT) legislation, processes, and initiatives

Past papers and practice questions

Students can access past papers for this module by logging into the MyICSA
area of www.icsaglobal.com.

Acronyms and abbreviations

AGM	annual general meeting
AIM	Alternative Investment Market
AML	anti-money laundering
APACS	Association for Payment Clearing Services
ARROW II	advanced risk responsive operating framework
ATE	After The Event (insurance)
ATM	automated teller machine
BACS	Bankers' Automated Clearing Services
BAILII	British and Irish Legal Information Institute
BCBS	Basel Committee on Banking Supervision
BIC	Bank Identification Code
CDD	customer due diligence
CFT	combating finance for terrorism
CGT	capital gains tax
CHAPS	Clearing House Automated Payment System
CHF	Swiss francs
DPA	Data Protection Act 1998
EC	European Community
EDD	enhanced due diligence
EU	European Union
EUSTD	European Savings Tax Directive (sometimes referred to as the EUSD)
FATF	Financial Action Task Force
FCA	Financial Conduct Authority
FEC	forward exchange contract
FIU	Financial Intelligence Unit
forex/FX	foreign exchange (market)
FSA	Financial Services Authority
FSMA	Financial Services and Markets Act 2000
G10	Group of 10
GBP	British pounds
GFCI	Global Financial Centres Index
GIFCS	Group of International Finance Centre Supervisors
HMRC	Her Majesty's Revenue & Customs
HNWI	high net worth individuals
IAIS	International Association of Insurance Supervisors
IBAN	international bank account number
ICSA	Institute of Chartered Secretaries and Administrators
IHT	inheritance tax
ILP	Incorporated Limited Partnership
IMF	International Monetary Fund
IOM	Isle of Man
IOSCO	International Organization of Securities Commissions
IRS	Internal Revenue Service
ISA	Individual Savings Account
ISO	International Organization for Standardization
IT	income tax
JMLSG	Joint Money Laundering Steering Group
KYC	know your customer
LDF	Liechtenstein Disclosure Facility
LLP	Limited Liability Partnership
LP	Limited Partnership
LSE	London Stock Exchange
LVCR	Low Value Consignment Relief
MLRO	Money Laundering Reporting Officer
MMOU	Multilateral Memorandum of Understanding
NCCT	non co-operating countries and territories
OECD	Organisation for Economic Co-operation and Development
OFAC	Office of Foreign Assets Control

OGIS	Offshore Group of Insurance Supervisors	SLP	Separate Limited Partnership
PCC	Protected Cell Company	SOCA	Serious Organised Crime Agency
PEP	politically exposed person	STEP	Society for Trust and Estate Practitioners
PET	Potentially Exempt Transfer	STR	suspicious transaction report
PIN	personal identification number	SWIFT	Society for Worldwide Interbank Financial Telecommunication
plc	public limited company	SYSC	Systems and Controls
PoCA	Proceeds of Crime Act 2002	TIEA	Tax Information Exchange Agreement
PRA	Prudential Regulation Authority	UKLA	UK Listing Authority
RBC	remittance basis charge	UN	United Nations
RDR	Retail Distribution Review	UNODC	United Nations Office on Drugs and Crime
RTGS	real time, gross settlement		
SAR	suspicious activity report	USD	US dollars
SEPA	Single European Payments Area	VAT	value added tax
SIB	Securities and Investments board (now the FSA)	VISR	Virgin Islands Shipping Registry

Acknowledgements

This study text was funded by the ICSA Education and Research Foundation.

Part One

Offshore centres and the offshore financial services sector

After studying this part, students will gain an understanding of the meaning of 'offshore' and will be able to identify some of the main uses and users of offshore centres. Students will be able to identify factors that may influence an investor's choice of jurisdiction and services provider when choosing to use an offshore centre. Factors such as the legal systems, the standard of regulation, the reputation, the confidentiality (or in some cases secrecy) provisions, the political environment and the taxation environment are all discussed. Students will gain an understanding of key terms used within the offshore financial services industry and of the various products and services available from within offshore centres (including trust company business products and services, insurance services, tax compliance and tax planning services, retail fund management and portfolio management).

Learning outcomes

At the end of this part, students will be able to:

◆ explain the meaning of 'offshore';

◆ understand the economic influences that allow offshore centres to continue to develop;

◆ explain the concept of onshore offshore centres;

◆ identify the main uses of offshore centres;

◆ understand who uses offshore centres;

◆ identify various offshore centres;

◆ identify and describe the typical features of offshore centres;

◆ identify factors that may influence the choice of jurisdiction when choosing an offshore centre;

◆ identify factors to be considered when choosing an offshore services provider;

◆ understand key terms used within the offshore financial services industry;

◆ discuss the trust and company business products available offshore;

◆ discuss the trust and company business administration services available offshore;

◆ discuss the role of the trust and company administrator;

◆ discuss offshore insurance services including captive insurance companies;

◆ discuss legal services available offshore;

◆ identify the two broad categories of tax compliance and tax planning;

◆ identify the two main areas of retail fund managers and private portfolio management; and

◆ discuss portfolio management services provided and basic portfolio planning considerations.

Chapter one
The development and features of offshore centres

List of topics

1. The development of the offshore industry
2. The users and uses of offshore centres
3. Various offshore centres
4. Typical features of offshore centres
5. Choosing an offshore centre
6. Choosing an offshore service provider

Introduction

This chapter explains what is meant by the terms 'offshore centre', 'low tax jurisdiction' and 'tax haven'. The typical features of an offshore centre are outlined, and some of the main users and uses of offshore centres are discussed as are various offshore centres. The chapter outlines some of the many considerations that may influence a **person's** choice of offshore centre and concludes by discussing some characteristics that many clients may seek when choosing an offshore services provider.

1. The development of the offshore industry

1.1 What is an offshore financial centre?

It is difficult to define exactly what an offshore financial centre (referred to as an **offshore centre** for the remainder of this text) is. An offshore centre could be described as a **jurisdiction** which provides much of its financial services business to non-residents and seeks to create a competitive advantage through its laws. However, this could also describe many, if not all, of the financial centres in the world, including that of London.

person
Used to refer to both natural persons such as individuals and legal persons (i.e. those that are created by law) such as companies.

offshore centre
A jurisdiction which seeks to create a competitive advantage through its laws and which provides financial services primarily to non-residents.

jurisdiction
A territory over which authority is exercised by laws which are under the control of a system of courts different to that of its neighbouring areas.

direct taxes
Taxes on income (e.g.
income tax).

The term 'onshore offshore' jurisdiction is used to describe jurisdictions such as the UK, Canada and the Netherlands which are major onshore jurisdictions that can be used by offshore residents for 'offshore' purposes due to the treatment that is applied to non-residents (e.g. they are exempt from **direct taxes**).

An International Monetary Fund (IMF) background paper on offshore financial centres, prepared in June 2000, explains that offshore centres are usually jurisdictions that:

◆ have relatively large numbers of financial institutions engaged primarily in business with non-residents;

◆ have financial systems with external assets and liabilities out of proportion to domestic financial intermediation designed to finance domestic economies; and

◆ provide some or all services such as low or zero taxation, moderate or light regulation, banking secrecy or anonymity.

Since the IMF paper was written, the regulation in many offshore centres has become comparable to that found in onshore jurisdictions, and the banking secrecy and anonymity provisions exist only for legitimate business. Nevertheless, in general, the above descriptions are useful when describing what an offshore centre is.

1.2 The development of offshore industries

There are various economic influences that allow offshore centres to continue to develop.

Onshore centres have, over the years, introduced anti-avoidance measures to make it more difficult for their residents to benefit from lower taxes by moving their finances offshore. Offshore centres have responded by continuously adapting, becoming more diverse and seeking new opportunities in order to remain competitive.

Offshore centres seek to be innovative in terms of the products that they offer and their legal environments. For example, in the last few years, common law offshore centres have introduced legislation allowing for the formation of foundations which appeal to clients from civil law countries where the concept of trusts is not widely recognised.

Over the years it has become far easier for clients to switch their business dealings between jurisdictions as the global financial market has become more accessible. Offshore centres have adapted in order to remain competitive with each other; for example, laws have been passed enabling companies to change easily the country under whose laws they are registered while maintaining the same legal identity (a process known as redomiciliation) and the offering of products and services offshore continues to expand.

Many jurisdictions are seeking to distance themselves from being described as 'offshore' as the term has become associated with negative stereotypes. Instead, many offshore jurisdictions are seeking to position themselves as 'International

Finance Centres' as opposed to 'Offshore Centres', a description which is in line with London and other major financial centres in the world, which are seen to be reputable, transparent, cooperative and acceptable places to do business with.

In the international community, it has been recognised that not all offshore centres are the same. International organisations such as Financial Action Task Force (FATF) now focus on whether or not individual centres comply with, or cooperate with, the implementation of international standards, rather than simply focussing on whether a jurisdiction is considered to be 'onshore' or 'offshore'.

Other terms which are used to describe offshore centres include 'low tax jurisdictions' and 'tax havens'.

1.3 Low tax jurisdictions

Low tax jurisdictions are those such as the Isle of Man, Jersey or Guernsey which have direct taxes (e.g. taxes on income) set at a rate that, compared with certain onshore jurisdictions, may be considered to be relatively low.

Many low tax jurisdictions are said to be 'tax havens' so far as non-residents are concerned, as these individuals are usually exempt from direct taxes that are applicable to individuals who are resident.

1.4 Tax havens

In 1998, the Organisation for Economic Co-operation and Development (OECD) used the term 'tax haven' in its report entitled 'Harmful Tax Competition: An Emerging Global Issue'. The report considered a number of factors, to decide whether a jurisdiction was a 'tax haven'; however, the key criteria included:

◆ no or only nominal taxes;
◆ lack of effective exchange of information;
◆ lack of transparency; and
◆ no substantial activity.

In 2000, the OECD published a list of over 40 jurisdictions that met the criteria for tax havens set out in the 1998 report. In mid 2002, it published a list of 'uncooperative tax havens' which did not make commitments to transparency and exchange of information.

The term 'tax haven' has taken on an increasingly negative meaning. It conjures thoughts of dishonest individuals or companies hiding their money and therefore illegally evading a tax liability in their own jurisdiction. Offshore centres that are described as tax havens attract a lot of undesirable attention from the international community and the media. Offshore centres have increasingly avoided being referred to as tax havens and many have taken steps to appear more transparent and cooperative.

In May 2009, the last three jurisdictions (Andorra, Liechtenstein and Monaco) were removed from the list in light of their commitments to implement the

OECD standards. The OECD's work on transparency and effective exchange of information is discussed further in Chapter 9.

The term 'tax havens' is sometimes used to describe jurisdictions where there are low or no direct taxes. Tax havens are also referred to as 'no-tax jurisdictions' or 'zero tax jurisdictions'. Offshore centres where there are no direct taxes are referred to as 'pure tax havens' (for example, Anguilla or the Bahamas). In tax havens, it is usual to find that **indirect taxes** (i.e. those that are on expenditure) are higher in order to create sufficient revenue for the government.

indirect taxes
Taxes on expenditure (e.g. VAT).

Test yourself 1.1

What is an offshore centre?

2. The users and uses of offshore centres

Many users of offshore centres are 'high net worth individuals' (HNWIs). The UK's Financial Services and Markets Act 2000 (Financial Promotion) Order 2005 describes an HNWI as someone who had an annual income to the value of £100,000 or more during the financial year or net assets of £250,000 or more (excluding primary residence). In offshore centres, however, the term is used to describe wealthy individuals who are usually advised by professional intermediaries such as tax advisers, accountants or lawyers. Different offshore service providers have their own definition of HNWIs.

The range of users of offshore centres includes individuals, entrepreneurs, small businesses, trading companies, multinational incorporations and charities. Anyone who wishes to secure an advantage that would not be available in their own jurisdiction – for example, protection from taxes or certainty over the future taxation policies of their governments – could seek to use an offshore centre.

The reasons for using offshore centres mainly stem from their features (e.g. low taxation) or from the products and services that are available offshore (trusts, companies, partnerships, etc.). These are discussed in section 4 of this chapter and in section 3 of Chapter 2 respectively.

The uses of offshore centres include:

◆ tax-efficient structuring of international trade and investment;
◆ private client wealth structuring;
◆ holding and investment companies;
◆ offshore investment funds;
◆ protection of personal wealth and estates;
◆ captive insurance companies;
◆ ship registration; and
◆ the managing of pension funds for employees of multinational corporations.

Tax efficiency is a common reason for individuals choosing to use offshore centres. Factors such as residence (where a person lives) and domicile (which is distinct from a person's residence and is where they truly feel at 'home') are often relevant in deciding whether or not individuals will be taxed in their country of residence and determine the basis of taxation to which an individual is subject. There are often opportunities for individuals who are domiciled in a different jurisdiction to that in which they are resident to use offshore centres to minimise a tax liability. For example, they may only be taxed in their country of residence on funds that they bring into that country and not on their 'worldwide' income, and taxes in offshore centres often do not apply to non-residents. A full discussion on tax planning concepts such as residence and domicile is included in Chapter 5.

3. Various offshore centres

There are many offshore centres and international finance centres.

3.1 The Crown Dependencies

The Crown Dependencies consist of the Bailiwick of Guernsey (which includes Alderney, with its own company legislation, and Sark), the Bailiwick of Jersey and the Isle of Man. They are self-governing jurisdictions that are not part of the UK and are not represented in the UK Parliament. They are legislatively independent from the UK and have autonomy in relation to their domestic affairs, including taxation.

The UK government is responsible for the international affairs and defence of the Crown Dependencies, although it will not act on behalf of the Crown Dependencies internationally or legislate for them without prior consultation. While they are separate from the UK, the Crown Dependencies have a close relationship with it and this has been a significant attraction for business. Much of the business conducted in the Crown Dependencies is UK-related.

The Crown Dependencies have their own legal systems which are a mixture of customary law and statute law. They make their own legislation; however, primary legislation passed requires royal assent from the Privy Council. This process ensures that there is no conflict with international obligations. While English law does not apply, the courts draw heavily on English common law in some areas. The statutory provisions are often modelled on English Acts of Parliament and where this is the case, English cases are frequently referenced by their courts. In some areas, the Crown Dependencies have adopted laws to meet their own special circumstances. The Judicial Committee of the Privy Council is the court of final appeal for the Crown Dependencies.

The Crown Dependencies are stable and well-regulated jurisdictions that are transparent and do not have statutory banking secrecy provisions.

Under the terms of Protocol 3 of the UK's 1972 Treaty of Accession to the European Communities, now the European Union (EU), the Crown Dependencies have a limited relationship with the EU and this allows for free movement of goods and trade within EU member states. The Crown

fiscal policies
Policies that relate to the
public revenues (i.e. income
from taxation).

Dependencies are not a part of the EU and its directives do not therefore apply. The Crown Dependencies are not required to harmonise their **fiscal policies** and legislative framework with those of EU member states, although the Isle of Man has chosen to become a part of the EU's value added tax (VAT) regime.

The British Crown Dependencies are not empowered to sign or ratify international conventions on their own behalf; however, the UK may extend the ratification of any convention to the Crown Dependencies. In some cases, they have done so, and in others similar requirements have been put in place in order to implement international regulatory standards and standards to combat anti-money laundering (AML) and combating finance for terrorism (CFT).

The Bailiwick of Jersey

Jersey is an island which is approximately nine miles by five. It is located approximately 85 miles from the English coast and 14 miles off the north-west coast of France. It has a population of approximately 90,800 people.

The main finance industry sectors in Jersey are the banking, fund administration and the trust company business sectors. Insurance business is not conducted on a significant scale from Jersey. There are many legal and accountancy practices that operate from within the island, supporting its finance industry.

The Bailiwick of Guernsey

The Bailiwick comprises the principal islands of Guernsey, Alderney and Sark together with other smaller islands. The Bailiwick of Guernsey is located in the English Channel, in the bay of St Malo off the north-west coast of France (very near Jersey). Guernsey's population is approximately 62,000, Alderney's population is approximately 2,000 and Sark's is 600.

The financial services industry in Guernsey includes banking, trust and fiduciary sectors, funds, insurance and asset management. Banking is central to the Bailiwick of Guernsey's finance industry and is a major source of employment in the Bailiwick. Guernsey is the leading captive insurance domicile in Europe in terms of numbers of captives and is fourth in the world, based on premiums written.

The Isle of Man

The Isle of Man (IOM) is 33 miles by 13 miles and is located in the middle of the Irish Sea. While the Isle of Man is a part of the British Isles, it is not a part of the UK. Its population is approximately 80,000.

legal persons
Those persons that are
incorporated by law
(e.g. companies).

Banking and insurance services represent the most significant financial service businesses in the IOM. Funds business has been a growing sector and the IOM has also licensed some online gambling businesses. The use of **legal persons** and arrangements such as trusts are also prevalent.

3.2 The British Overseas Territories

The constitutional relationship of British Overseas Territories is quite different to that of the Crown Dependencies.

Offshore centres such as Anguilla, Bermuda, the British Virgin Islands, the Cayman Islands, Gibraltar, Montserrat and the Turks and Caicos Islands are all British Overseas Territories.

Gibraltar

Gibraltar is an overseas territory of the United Kingdom. It is not an island. It is situated on the peninsula at the southern tip of Spain, just opposite the north coast of Africa. Its population is approximately 30,000.

Gibraltar is a self-governing British Overseas Territory which has been a constituent of the EU since 1973 under the UK Treaty of Accession as it is a European territory whose external relations are the responsibility of an EU member state. However, it is excluded from the common external tariff, the common agricultural policy, and the requirement to levy VAT.

Financial services are a significant part of Gibraltar's economy and include banking, insurance, trust and company business and fund management including collective investment schemes.

British Virgin Islands

The Territory of the British Virgin Islands is a non-self-governing overseas territory of the UK. The territory is located within the Virgin Islands archipelago a few miles east of the United States Virgin Islands. It consists of approximately 60 islands, islets and cays, 20 of which are inhabited. The capital of the Virgin Islands is Road Town which is situated on the largest island, Tortola. This island is approximately 13.5 miles long and 3 miles wide, and is the home of approximately 22,900 persons of a total population of 27,518.

The financial services sector is significant to the British Virgin Islands economy. Services such as accountancy, banking and legal services, Captive Insurance, company incorporations, mutual funds administration and trust formation are all provided from within the British Virgin Islands. The Virgin Islands are regarded as being among the world's leading domiciles for hedge funds and the Territory has also sustained substantial growth in the areas of captive insurance companies. In addition, the UK government launched the Virgin Islands Shipping Registry (VISR) in 2006, which enabled the Territory to be upgraded to a Category 1 Shipping Registry.

The Virgin Islands have locally enacted legislation and imperial legislation which is enacted by order of Her Majesty and with the advice of the Privy Council. The common law of England also applies. The Judicial Committee of the Privy Council is the final court of appeal for the British Virgin Islands.

3.3 Mainland countries

Offshore centres include some mainland countries such as Monaco, which is surrounded on three sides by France and lies on the coast of the Mediterranean Sea, Panama, which is the southern-most country of Central America, and Liechtenstein, which is a landlocked country in Central Europe (although it is not a part of the EU).

3.4 Other offshore centres

The Bahamas, Barbados, Belize, the Commonwealth of Dominica, St Kitts and Nevis (both parts of this Federation have separate company and trust litigation), St Lucia, St Vincent, the Grenadines, Cyprus, Malta, the Seychelles, Curacao (part of the Netherlands Antilles) and Aruba are all offshore centres as well as the Republic of Mauritius.

The Republic of Mauritius

The Republic of Mauritius consists of the islands of Mauritius (main island), Rodrigues, Agalega, St Brandon, and the Chagos Archipelago. The Republic of Mauritius obtained its independence from the British in 1968 and became a Republic on 12 March 1992. The population of Mauritius numbers around 1.2 million people. English is the official language; however, French is also widely used.

Mauritius is a member of the Commonwealth, the United Nations and related organisations, the Organisation of African Unity, and the Indian Ocean Commission.

The financial sector in Mauritius is a growing sector and consists of banking business, insurance companies, stock market and other financial intermediaries. The banking sector is the largest. There are no bank secrecy laws that apply to banks in Mauritius.

structure
Used to describe a group of trusts and companies that are connected by their ownership or their assets and are aimed at meeting the needs of a particular client or group of clients.

The Mauritian legal system is largely based on English and French law. Criminal procedure law is mainly English, while the Criminal Code was influenced by the French Code and the civil law is modelled on the Napoleonic Code. The ultimate court of appeal is the Judicial Committee of the Privy Council in England.

Test yourself 1.2

State three uses of offshore centres.

exchange control regulations
Regulations or other controls that are imposed by the governments of some countries that fear or are experiencing scarcity of foreign currency (and often, precious metals). Such controls may limit or ban the amount of foreign or local currency that can be traded or purchased, or may involve controls which restrict residents from removing currency out of the jurisdiction.

4. Typical features of offshore centres

Features of a typical offshore centre may include:

◆ low or zero taxation (or exemption for non-residents);

◆ no tax on profits or wealth taxes or capital gains taxes;

◆ moderate or light regulation;

◆ privacy and confidentiality provisions;

◆ reduced requirements for disclosure of information to the authorities;

◆ widely available asset protection **structures** such as trusts and companies;

◆ the availability of a high level of financial expertise; and

◆ a lack of **exchange control regulations**.

Exchange control regulations are regulations or other controls that are imposed by the governments of some countries that fear or are experiencing scarcity of foreign currency (and often, precious metals). Such controls may limit or ban the amount of foreign or local currency that can be traded or purchased or may involve controls which restrict residents from removing currency out of the jurisdiction.

Stop and think 1.1

Which of the typical features of offshore centres are present in your own jurisdiction?

5. Choosing an offshore centre

There are a number of factors which may influence a person's choice of offshore centre, including:

◆ their country of residence;

◆ where they wish to retire;

◆ their business and intended activities;

◆ their short-term and long-term objectives;

◆ their reasons for using an offshore centre; and

◆ the content of any tax or legal advice that they may have received.

While there are typical features of offshore centres, there are differences between them which may influence a client's choice. These differences can be due to the niche markets that have developed the characteristics of the legal system, the standard of regulation, the reputation, the confidentiality and privacy provisions, the political infrastructure, the taxation environment and the physical and human infrastructure of an offshore centre.

5.1 Niche markets

Many offshore centres have developed niche positions in the international markets and the activity with which the client is involved may therefore influence their choice of jurisdiction. Guernsey, for example, has a very established captive insurance market.

Specialised services such as compliant Islamic financial services may be offered in the key financial sectors in some offshore centres and for some clients this will be a relevant consideration when choosing an offshore centre.

Making it work 1.1: Niche markets

In December 2008, the Chancellor of the Exchequer commissioned Michael Foot to undertake a review of the British Crown Dependencies (Guernsey, Isle of Man and Jersey) and six overseas territories (Anguilla, Bermuda, the British Virgin Islands, the Cayman Islands, Gibraltar and Turks and Caicos Islands) in order to identify the opportunities and challenges facing them. The review was published on 29 October 2009 and identified the various niche positions in international markets for some of the jurisdictions under review.

The **Cayman Islands** are the world's leading centre for hedge funds and also have a significant wholesale banking centre, with high volumes of overnight banking business from the USA.

Bermuda is the third largest reinsurance centre in the world and the second largest captive insurance domicile, with firms based in the jurisdiction writing significant volumes of business in the UK and the USA.

The **British Virgin Islands** are the leading domicile for international business companies, with much business coming from the Far East in addition to strong business links with the USA.

Gibraltar offers a gateway to the European single market.

The **Crown Dependencies** provide a gateway to route funds to other financial centres, including London; they also service the financial needs of many UK nationals living abroad.

5.2 Legal systems

The following are considerations relating to the legal system that may influence a person's choice of offshore centre.

The familiarity of the legislation

Offshore centres which have laws that are similar to English company law, for example, will appeal to those who are familiar with that law. In some offshore centres, such as Mauritius, the highest court of appeal is the Privy Council in the UK and this will offer some comfort.

The flexibility of the laws

Company laws that are flexible and not too prescriptive enable the provisions of onshore legislation to be incorporated into the articles of association of a company to replicate that law.

A lack of exchange control regulations

A lack of exchange control regulations that allow freedom of movement of funds in and out of the jurisdiction is desirable.

The range of entities available

Legislation in some offshore centres now provides for a range of **entities** such as limited liability partnerships, separate limited partnerships, incorporated limited partnerships, protected cell companies, incorporated cell companies and foundations as well as the more traditional trusts and limited liability companies.

entities
Used to describe both legal persons (such as companies) and legal arrangements (such as trusts).

Responsiveness

The legislation, processes and infrastructure in an offshore centre should allow it to respond quickly in order to meet the client's needs and expectations. Jurisdictions such as Jersey now offer 'fast track' incorporations which mean that a company could be incorporated within the timeframe of two hours. Guernsey can offer incorporations within 15 minutes where the purpose of the company is a simple asset holding company and where the standard memorandum and articles are used.

Access to stock exchanges

Whether the shares of companies incorporated within the jurisdiction can be traded on major stock exchanges, such as the London Stock Exchange (LSE), the NASDAQ, Alternative Investment Market (AIM), the Hong Kong stock exchange etc., or the ability to issue uncertified securities enabling electronic trading of the shares through CREST. Jersey, for example, has legislation that facilitates this whereas the Caribbean jurisdictions do not.

Administrative requirements

Some jurisdictions, such as Jersey, allow for the requirement for annual general meetings (AGMs) to be waived, whereas others do not. Some offshore centres require financial statements for private companies to be audited whereas others only require them to be filed. In the Isle of Man, the Registrar of Companies must be informed whenever there is a change in the officers of the company. Offshore centres with fewer administrative requirements will allow costs to be kept to a minimum.

Asset protection legislation

Upon the death of individuals in some jurisdictions, the legislation of the jurisdiction provides that their assets must be distributed in accordance with the provisions set out in those laws. The rules are referred to as **forced heirship** rules. The legislation should provide for protection against forced heirship rules.

forced heirship
In some countries, the laws require the assets held in a person's estate to pass to stated heirs (usually the person's spouse and children). This is known as forced heirship and such heirs are known as 'forced heirs' (or sometimes 'fixed heirs').

Independence

The local legislature and judiciary need to be able to operate independently and free of government interference.

5.3 Regulation

The global financial crisis has highlighted the need for high standards of financial sector regulation and supervision. Characteristics of offshore centres that operate such standards may include:

◆ operating with a depositor compensation scheme;

◆ operating standards that are in line with international standards such as the third AML EU directive and the FATF recommendations. Offshore centres which are able to score comparatively or better than the onshore jurisdictions help to highlight misconceptions about the way in which many offshore centres operate;

◆ having a track record of operating within the supervisory regime for many years; and

◆ being highly rated by the IMF or members of respected international bodies such as the International Organization of Securities Commissions (IOSCO), the Group of International Finance Centre Supervisors (formerly the offshore group of banking supervisors).

5.4 Reputation

The reputation of the offshore centre is extremely important. Clients who deal with jurisdictions that appear on any 'blacklist' may find it increasingly difficult to deal outside of this jurisdiction. The following is a non-exhaustive list of factors that could be considered when assessing the reputation of an offshore centre.

◆ Inclusion on the OECD 'white list' meaning that the jurisdiction has implemented internationally agreed tax standards along with onshore jurisdictions such as the UK, France and the USA.

◆ Comprehensive and wide-reaching Tax Information Exchange Agreements (TIEAs).

◆ The jurisdictions rating in the Global Financial Centres Index (GFCI).

◆ The level of compliance with the FATF 40+9 recommendations.

5.5 Confidentiality and privacy provisions

An offshore centre should protect the privacy and confidentiality of financial information for legitimate business activities while remaining committed to the international fight against financial crime such as money laundering and financing of terrorism.

The requirements to report information to the authorities differ from jurisdiction to jurisdiction. For example, it is a requirement in some jurisdictions to disclose the beneficial ownership of companies at the time of incorporation only, whereas in others there is an ongoing requirement. In some offshore centres there is a central registry of trusts, whereas in others no public information on trusts is held.

Many offshore centres have signed TIEAs with other jurisdictions in order to comply with the OECD's international agreement, based on the OECD's model agreement. These TIEAs mean that in certain circumstances, information may be exchanged where a person is under investigation for fiscal crime in a jurisdiction. The OECD and tax information exchange agreements are discussed further in Chapter 7.

Many offshore centres have data protection legislation in line with that of the UK.

Some offshore centres have strict banking secrecy laws; however, these have attracted negative publicity and have been subject to increased attention from governments in onshore jurisdictions and the OECD.

Making it work 1.2: The US government and UBS

In 2008, the US government alleged that Switzerland's largest bank, UBS, had defrauded US tax authorities between 2006 and 2007 by creating complex offshore structures for their clients in which they could hide their assets from the Internal Revenue Service (IRS), which collects taxes for the US government.

Despite Switzerland's strict bank secrecy laws, in February 2009, UBS agreed to pay $780m (£549m) to the US government and Switzerland's regulator ordered UBS to hand over the identities of approximately 250–300 clients.

Many were shocked by the decision of the Swiss authorities. Swiss President and Finance Minister Hans-Rudolf Merz was widely reported to have indicated that if UBS had failed to meet the deadlines set by the US authorities, this could have led to the loss of its US operating licence and this would have threatened the very existence of the bank, and with it, the Swiss economy.

Immediately after above events in February 2009, the US filed a new civil lawsuit, demanding that UBS hand over information on 52,000 US account holders. Switzerland recognises tax fraud as a crime (and would have been in a position to release information if a client had committed this offence), but not tax evasion (which was the focus of the allegations). UBS therefore faced breaking US tax laws if it did not disclose the details and breaking Swiss secrecy laws if it did.

In August 2009, the Swiss government negotiated on behalf of the bank and, in order to end the dispute, an agreement was signed whereby UBS agreed to give the US tax authorities the details of 4,450 accounts of customers who were most suspected of tax evasion.

As well as the releasing of the information, international pressure has caused Switzerland to sign up to the OECD international standards to facilitate exchange of information, having previously stated that the rules would compromise its long-standing banking secrecy principles. Commentators have stated that this is the beginning of the end of bank secrecy legislation.

5.6 Political infrastructure

The political infrastructure of an offshore centre is of utmost importance. Potential investors in an offshore centre will want to be certain that the offshore centre is politically, socially and economically stable and free from problems such as war and corruption. Political control must be clearly in the hands of the governing party. The government should have high moral standards and should not allow organised criminals to operate from within its jurisdiction.

A strong local economy is preferable with a good standard of living and an absence of civil unrest. It is important that the government can operate autonomously and, if it is an overseas territory, there should be restricted ability of the mother country to intervene. The political environment in an offshore centre should not make the costs of operating from within the offshore centre excessive.

5.7 Tax environment

A tax environment that has been stable for number of years offers certainty that, for example, some feel is not present in the UK under the current government.

Desirable features of an offshore centre's tax environment include:

◆ no corporation taxes (or nominal corporation taxes);
◆ competitive initial registration and winding-up taxes;
◆ competitive stamp duties;
◆ no stamp duty on incorporated holding companies;
◆ no income taxes;
◆ no capital gains taxes;
◆ no VAT;
◆ no withholding taxes on payment of dividends or interest paid on loans;
◆ no wealth taxes;
◆ no inheritance taxes;
◆ a Double Taxation Agreement network;
◆ scope for tax deferral;
◆ the existence of a network of double taxation agreements.

5.8 Physical infrastructure

Desirable features of the physical infrastructure of an offshore centre include:

◆ operating in the same time zone as major centres (for example, Jersey, Guernsey and the Isle of Man all operate within the same time zone as the UK and the Caribbean jurisdictions operate within the same time zone as New York);
◆ being located close to a major onshore centre and having direct flights to major centres on a frequent basis, as this allows easy access for clients and their advisers;

◆ having an attractive climate and environment with good accommodation for clients and their advisers and offshore centres with a good tourist industry may have an advantage;

◆ the presence within the jurisdiction of major accountancy firms and legal practices;

◆ the presence of a large number of international banks within the offshore centre; and

◆ a comprehensive and robust information technology infrastructure.

5.9 Human infrastructure

The presence of a large number of finance industry professionals including those with experience and qualifications within banking, trusts and company administration, fund administration and management, accountancy and legal sectors is desirable.

The spoken language in a jurisdiction could also be an important factor for the client. Mauritius, for example, has a population which is bilingual (French and English).

Test yourself 1.3

a) **What factors might influence an individual's choice of offshore centre?**

b) **State two desirable characteristics of a legal system in an offshore centre.**

---

6. Choosing an offshore service provider

The range of service providers offshore is vast.

Few clients today simply call a service provider as a result of their own research or via a service provider's website. In fact, in well-regulated jurisdictions, service providers would exercise caution where clients do contact them in this way. Instead, clients are very often introduced to service providers either because they are already a client of a part of the group or through an intermediary such as a lawyer, tax adviser or banker. Often, offshore service providers are asked by intermediaries or introducers to attend a 'beauty parade' where they explain the services that they can provide and compete with other service providers for a client's business.

The choice of service provider will depend to some extent on the aims of the client, the resources available to them and their client service expectations. Different clients seek different qualities in a service provider for a variety of reasons.

A client looking to settle a trust may wish for their trustee to be provided by a trust company that is entirely independent. In this case, they may seek an independent trust company and avoid those which are bank-owned or offer their own portfolio management services.

Other clients may prefer to keep their business confined to entities which are connected – for example with their existing bankers. It is not uncommon for banks to own trust companies and to be able to keep the provision of bank accounts, a trustee, portfolio managers and other advisers in-house. The lack of independence may mean that the bank-owned company is unlikely to choose external parties to provide services to the trust (even if they may offer better rates of interest, for example). However, it can be argued that the ability to provide services in-house outweighs the benefit of having such independence, securing lower fees for the client, creating operational efficiencies and the ability to know and understand all aspects of the client's business, thus creating opportunities for the client (as well as the bank).

Trust company business services, for example, may be provided by banks, bank-owned trust companies, law firm-owned trust companies, accountancy firms or independently owned trust companies. These range in terms of size from very small to very large organisations. A client with complicated structures spanning across jurisdictions may wish for their trustee to be a law firm with a presence in several jurisdictions, while a client whose main aim is to provide for their family after their own death may choose a 'family office' or small provider with whom they may build up a close relationship.

There are certain characteristics, however, that many clients will desire from their service provider and these include the following.

◆   Service providers should be regulated. A trustee who is asked to transfer a trust to a new service provider should ensure that they are comfortable that it is in the best interest of the client to do so. Such a provider will be conducting 'unauthorised' business in many jurisdictions and the client will not be afforded the usual protections that arise when dealing with trustees who are regulated and supervised.

◆   The service provider should be qualified and experienced at providing the services for which they are employed. Any marketing material should be accurate and not misleading in any way. The size of the service provider should be suitable for the client in that it should be such that the client feels that their business is important to the organisation.

◆   Some clients enjoy the security that being connected with a large institution may afford them, whereas others may prefer to be looked after by a small company where the staff know their business and where they receive a personal service.

◆   The fees and charges levied by the provider should be reasonable and transparent.

◆   The provider should be a reputable person and there should be a lack of adverse publicity about the provider and a good regulatory track record. A service provider's reputation is key to its ability to attract and retain good-quality clients and intermediary contacts.

◆   There should be a good level of customer service.

◆ The availability of talented and experienced professional staff (particularly those with experience of dealing with the jurisdiction or activity with which the client is connected) is desirable. Clients favour consistency and the ability to liaise with the same members of staff over time. High levels of staff turnover are not therefore appreciated.

◆ Service providers should be efficient. Some service providers take a risk-based approach to account opening and new client take-on procedures whereby the process is kept as simple and proportionate as possible. Other organisations may be more cautious and insist on more stringent requirements that increase the level of fees charged to the client and which take longer to adhere to.

◆ The compatibility of the investment philosophies of the client and the service provider should be considered. Some clients, for example, may seek Sharia-compliant structures.

The desirability of service providers to act for any given client will limit the choice of service providers available to them. For example:

◆ some service providers are willing to provide services to clients who present a higher risk to their business than others;

◆ some will not provide limited services such as 'providing a registered office only' (seeking to retain full control over the activities of the entities that they administer);

◆ some will not provide services to clients located in higher-risk jurisdictions or partaking in higher-risk activities;

◆ some require a minimum investment; and

◆ the service provider may not be authorised to provide the service under its financial services business licence.

Less scrupulous clients will seek service providers with the opposite characteristics to those usually desired. They will seek, for example, providers where the staff do not understand the business and will accept whatever business opportunities they are presented with. Some of the more usual concerns – for example, the fees and charges levied by the provider – may be of minimal importance to these individuals.

Test yourself 1.4

What factors might a potential user of an offshore service provider take into consideration when choosing a service provider?

Chapter summary

◆ An offshore centre is any jurisdiction (whether an island or not) which has a relatively large number of financial institutions which are engaged primarily in business with non-residents and which provides other benefits – for example, low taxation. Offshore business is simply the provision of financial services to non-residents.

◆ The term 'offshore' together with the term 'tax havens' have taken on negative meanings and many offshore centres have therefore sought to position themselves as international finance centres.

◆ The range of users of offshore centres includes wealthy individuals (HNWIs), as well as multinational incorporations, all of which seek to secure an advantage that would not be available to them from within their own jurisdiction.

◆ Typical features of offshore centres may include low or zero taxation, no wealth taxes or capital gains taxes, privacy and confidentiality provisions, reduced disclosure requirements to the authorities, availability of a high level of financial expertise and a lack of exchange control regulations.

◆ The factors which may influence a person's choice of offshore centre could include their personal ambitions, the characteristics of the legal system, the standard of the regulation, the reputation, confidentiality provisions, taxation environment, the political, physical and human infrastructure of an offshore centre.

◆ The size, independence, range of services available, reputation and charges may all be relevant considerations when choosing a service provider from the vast range of providers available.

Chapter two
Offshore financial services

List of topics

1. The offshore financial services sector
2. Key terms defined
3. Trust and company products available offshore
4. Trust company business services available offshore
5. Trust and company administration
6. Offshore insurance services
7. Legal services available in offshore centres
8. Tax compliance and tax planning
9. Investment management services

Introduction

This chapter discusses the financial services that are typically offered in offshore centres. Key terms that are often used in the finance industry are explained. The chapter explains some of the trust and company business products that are available offshore, including trusts, companies, foundations and a variety of partnerships. Trust company business services provided in connection with the products are discussed as is the role of the trust and company administrator. The advantages of captive insurance companies are discussed, as are legal and taxation services that are available in offshore centres. The chapter concludes with a discussion regarding the types of investment management services that are available offshore and some factors that should be considered when planning an investment portfolio.

1. The offshore financial services sector

The financial services sector in an offshore centre may typically offer the provision of the following services:

◆ trust company business services;

◆ insurance services;

◆ investment management services;

◆ legal services; and

◆ tax compliance and tax planning services.

financial services business
Used to describe the carrying on of investment business, trust company business, general insurance mediation business, money services business or funds services business.

The term **financial services business** is used to describe the carrying on of investment business, trust company business, general insurance mediation business, money service business or funds service business. An organisation that provides financial services business is often referred to as a **service provider**.

In many offshore jurisdictions, the provision of financial services business is a regulated activity that may not be carried on except by a business that has been issued with the relevant licence and is supervised by its regulator.

service provider
Organisations or individuals who provide financial services business offshore may simply be referred to as service providers.

2. Key terms defined

2.1 Fiduciary relationship

fiduciary relationship
A relationship founded on trust. A person with a fiduciary duty has a duty to act in the best interests of another person.

A **fiduciary relationship** is one that is founded on trust. A person with a fiduciary duty has a duty to act in the best interests of another person. A trustee, for example, has a fiduciary duty to act in the best interests of the beneficiaries of the trust, rather than acting in their own best interests.

2.2 Client

The term 'client' usually refers to the person who approached the offshore services provider in order to establish a business relationship. This is not, however, always the case. A trust company may use the term client to describe the settlor of a trust even though that person may not be a beneficiary; however, they could also use the term to describe a principal beneficiary who was not the provider of the funds or involved at the outset of the relationship.

2.3 Entities

legal arrangements
Legal arrangements include fiduciary arrangements such as trusts.

The term 'entities' is used to describe both legal persons (such as companies) and **legal arrangements** (such as trusts). Rather than referring to trusts, companies, foundations, partnerships etc., a trust company will simply refer to 'entities' under administration.

2.4 Structures

All of the entities that are aimed at meeting the needs of a particular client or group of clients and that are connected by virtue of their ownership or their assets are referred to collectively as the structure.

A structure may be very simple – for example, a company owned directly by a trust – or could be very complex – for example, multilayered, spanning across jurisdictions and including a range of different types of entities.

2.5 Overlying trusts / underlying companies

It is not uncommon for trusts and companies to be used together as a part of a client's tax or wealth planning. For example, a trust may own 100% of the share capital of a company. In this case, the trust would be referred to as an 'overlying trust' and the company would be referred to as an 'underlying company'. If the underlying company acquired the entire share capital of another company, it would then become the 'overlying company' of that new entity.

2.6 Trust company

A trust company is an organisation which conducts trust company business. The term usually refers to an organisation which offers the full range of trust company business services (described in section 4 of this chapter) although it is not uncommon for organisations such as accountancy firms to provide some limited services, such as company formations or the provision of a registered office.

Trust companies may be small or very large organisations owned by legal practices, major international banks, public companies or accountancy practices, or they may be owned by experienced individuals.

2.7 Service provider

Organisations or individuals that provide financial services business offshore may simply be referred to as service providers.

Test yourself 2.1

Give one example of a 'fiduciary relationship'.

3. Trust and company products available offshore

The main trust and company products offshore include trusts, companies, foundations and partnerships.

3.1 Trusts

A trust is a legal arrangement whereby a person (known as the settlor) properly vests (transfers in the correct manner) the legal ownership of assets (later referred to as the trust fund) to another person (known as the trustee) for the benefit of another person or persons (the beneficiaries).

The separation of the legal ownership (which lies with the trustee) of the trust fund and the equitable ownership (which lies with the beneficiaries) has many uses in financial planning.

A trust is not a corporate body and thus has no separate legal personality. The trustee therefore contracts in its name in its capacity as trustee. In the offshore environment, the trustee is usually a limited liability company. The terms of a trust depend on the type of trust and are set out in a private document known as a trust deed or a declaration of trust.

Trusts may be 'discretionary' trusts where the trustee is given absolute discretion as to who (from the class of beneficiaries described in the trust deed) will benefit from the trust and in what proportions, if at all. Life interest trusts (also known as interest in possession trusts) are those where a beneficiary referred to as the 'life tenant' has an absolute right to enjoy the income arising from the trust property during their lifetime and only on their death may the other beneficiaries (referred to as the remainder-men) stand to benefit. In essence, the life interest trust reverts to a discretionary trust upon the death of the life tenant.

The following are the most usual reasons for creating an offshore trust.

◆ To reduce a tax liability. For example, if assets have been settled into a trust, they do not form a part of an individual's estate upon their death and therefore the inheritance tax (IHT) charge may be avoided, provided they were settled into the trust more than seven years before the death of the settlor and that there were no gifts with reservation.

◆ To preserve confidentiality.

◆ To place assets in a safe jurisdiction.

◆ When emigrating or temporarily working abroad. An individual migrating to a high tax country can benefit by the setup of a pre-migration trust prior to taking up residence in the new country.

◆ To assist with an individual's estate planning prior to their death. The assets are administered by a professional trustee until they are distributed to the beneficiaries of the trust on the death of the settlor. This avoids the delay that is often experienced where executives are involved in disposing of assets.

◆ To hold property for minors.

◆ To protect family property from dissipation.

◆ To protect capital in the event of the beneficiary's financial difficulty or bankruptcy.

◆ To hold funds for a person who is incapable of looking after their financial affairs.

◆ To hold shares for employees, or provide for their pension in a tax-efficient manner.

◆ To hold funds for charitable purposes.

Test yourself 2.2

Identify three uses of an offshore trust.

3.2 Companies

There are many types of companies including limited liability companies, unlimited companies, those that are limited by guarantee, Protected Cell Companies and incorporated cell companies.

Limited liability companies

A company is an association of people who come together usually for business or profit-making purposes. A company comes into existence when it is incorporated by law. Upon incorporation, a company has a separate legal personality which is distinct from that of its shareholders and directors (e.g. it can sue and be sued in its own name). A company therefore enters into transactions in its own name and purchases assets in its own name.

A company is owned by its shareholders (also known as members) and is managed and controlled by its directors. The memorandum and articles of association set out the company's constitution. The memorandum sets out the name of the company, whether it is public and the authorised share capital. The articles of a company set out the rights and obligations of the shareholders.

Companies offer a number of benefits. For example, with a limited liability company, the liability of the shareholders is limited to the amount that they owe the company in respect of unpaid shares. Companies offer perpetual succession (they continue to exist in the event of the death of the shareholders or directors).

Uses of companies incorporated in offshore centres include for:

◆ holding investment portfolios;
◆ trading purposes;
◆ holding real estate;
◆ holding intellectual property rights; and
◆ holding assets such as yachts and aircrafts.

Unlimited companies

Unlimited companies differ from limited liability companies as the liability of the shareholders is unlimited (i.e. it is not limited to the amount that the shareholders owe the company by way of unpaid shares). These companies are not nearly as common as those that offer limited liability. In certain jurisdictions, the disclosure requirements are less than those of limited liability companies and this is attractive to some clients of offshore service providers.

Companies that are limited by guarantee

The liability of shareholders of companies that are limited by guarantee is limited to the amount which they undertake to pay in the event the winding up of the company. These companies are often used for not-for-profit purposes.

Protected Cell Companies

Guernsey was at the forefront of the development of Protected Cell Companies (PCCs) in the late 1990s. The motivation behind the development was to attract captive insurance work to Guernsey. The Isle of Man and the Cayman Islands both introduced PCC legislation, based on the Guernsey product. The Jersey model differs slightly.

Protected cells do not have their own legal personality. Where a protected cell wishes to contract, it does so by the cell company acting on its behalf. In some jurisdictions, such as Jersey, cells are treated as though they are a company for all other aspects of company law; for example, each cell must file an annual return as if it were a legal person. The cell company is responsible for the upkeep of each of its cells.

Each cell has its own constitution and members. A person is not a member of a cell company by virtue of being a member of a cell. The legislation could require that the directors, secretary and registered office of the cells are the same as those of the cell company. Guernsey, for example, imposes this requirement whereas Jersey allows the directors of the cell company to differ from those of the cell. The constitution ensures that the cell company retains ultimate control of the cells.

The key principle behind PCCs is that the assets and liabilities of a cell can be segregated, ring-fencing them. This means that the assets of a cell should only be available to creditors and shareholders of that cell.

Many offshore centres limit the use of PCCs. Typically, they may only be used in collective investment funds, insurance and securitisation structures. Jersey does not limit the use of PCCs.

PCCs are a popular vehicle in the captive insurance industry as they enable different insurers and classes of investors to benefit from shared overhead costs without losing protection from insolvency of the other cells.

PCCs are attractive vehicles for use in 'umbrella fund' investment schemes and collective investment funds. Using a PCC, a framework can be established, including all of the participants (manager, administrators and custodians). The documentation, once in place, can then easily be replicated upon the creation of a new cell. In addition, for those cell companies that require regulatory consent, this can be obtained in respect of one arrangement and then obtaining regulatory approval for further cells is a simplified matter. This ability to replicate a structure creates a clear commercial advantage.

Incorporated cells
Incorporated cells are a newer type of cell company whereby each 'incorporated cell' has its own separate legal identity. This makes it simpler for each cell to enter contracts and gives investors in jurisdictions not familiar with the concept of protected cells the comfort that their assets are ring-fenced adequately.

3.3 Foundations

Foundations have similar features to both trusts and companies. Foundations have a separate legal personality in the same way that companies do and can therefore contract in their own name. Foundations do not, however, have shareholders. General features of foundations include the following.

The person who requests for the foundation to be incorporated is the 'founder'. The Council administers the foundation and carries out its objects in accordance with the Charter and Regulations.

Some offshore centres impose restrictions on the council members and others do not. For example, Jersey requires that each council must have a 'qualified' member (one whose financial services business licence permits them to act in relation to foundations) and the application for a foundation to be incorporated must be lodged by a 'qualified' person. Liechtenstein foundations require a minimum of one member to be resident and qualified in Liechtenstein, whereas in Panama there are no such restrictions.

The foundation is governed by a Charter and Regulations. The Charter is usually available for public inspection and sets out the name of the foundation, its duration, objects and names and addresses of the first council members. The regulations are a private document setting out the administration of the foundation.

Unless the Charter or the regulations expressly provide, the beneficiaries have no interest in the foundation assets and are not owed a fiduciary duty by the foundation Council. This is very different to the duty owed by the trustee of a trust. This means that the constitution of the foundation can be drafted more flexibly than would otherwise be possible. The foundation may exist with no beneficiaries, whereas a trust may not.

In offshore centres such as Panama, foundations may have a guardian whereas in others such as Jersey, they *must* have a guardian to oversee the administration and ensure that the council carries on its functions properly.

Foundations have been used extensively in jurisdictions such as Panama and Liechtenstein for some time. The foundations legislation in Jersey has been in force from 17 July 2009. The government in Guernsey is in the process of preparing its foundations law which it hopes will be attractive to clients based in civil law jurisdictions in Europe and from emerging markets where the trust concept is less familiar than in common law countries. The Isle of Man is similarly in the process of introducing foundations legislation.

The benefits and uses of foundations include the following.

◆ Foundations appeal to clients who are involved with jurisdictions where the concept of trusts is less well known.
◆ Foundations offer an enhanced level of confidentiality.
◆ Global charities may use foundations for making donations.
◆ Clients may wish to use foundations within commercial transactions, especially where an 'orphaned' special purpose vehicle is required.
◆ Foundations can be used for international structuring.

3.4 Partnerships

A variety of types of partnerships are offered in offshore centres. General partnerships have been available for many years; however, others such as the

Incorporated Limited Partnership and the Separate Limited Partnership are relatively recent developments.

General partnerships

A general partnership is not an incorporated body and has no separate legal personality. The liability of partners of a general partnership (also known as a traditional partnership) is unlimited. A general partnership would be immediately dissolved on the death of one of the partners.

Limited Liability Partnerships

Limited Liability Partnerships (LLPs) are not corporate bodies; however, they do have a separate legal personality from that of their partners. It is the partnership itself that is responsible for any debts that it runs up rather than the individual partners and this is the attraction of this vehicle for many accountancy firms and other businesses. The liability of the partners (referred to as members, in the UK) is limited to the amount that they have contributed to the capital of the LLP.

Limited Partnerships

Limited Partnerships (LPs) are not corporate bodies and have no separate legal personality. LPs must have at least two types of partners; a limited partner (whose liability is limited to the amount of its capital contribution provided it does not take part in the management of the partnership) and a general partner (whose liability is unlimited).

Incorporated Limited Partnerships

Incorporated Limited Partnerships (ILPs) are the same as general partnerships, however; an ILP is a corporate body and therefore has a separate legal personality from that of its partners. An ILP therefore holds assets and contracts in its own name. The general partner is responsible for managing the assets of the partnership and owes fiduciary duties to the partnership analogous to those owed by a director to a company. As it is a corporate body, it offers the benefit of perpetual succession.

The general partner's liability remains unlimited for the debts of the ILP; however, the general partner acts as an agent of the partnership and is only liable for the debts that have not already been satisfied from the assets of the ILP. In practice, however, the liability of those persons managing the general partner can be limited by structuring the general partner as a limited company or limited partnership.

Separate Limited Partnerships

Separate Limited Partnerships (SLPs) are similar to limited partnerships as they have a separate legal personality; however, they are not a corporate body. In all other respects, an SLP is the same as a traditional partnership.

The general partner's liability remains unlimited; however, the general partner acts as an agent of the partnership and is only liable for the debts that have not already been satisfied from the assets of the SLP. As with an ILP, it is usual for the general partner to be a limited liability company.

ILPs and SLPs offer a greater degree of operational flexibility than corporate structures (particularly where investment capital may be returned to investors), while still retaining the additional protection and certainty that an LLP provides. ILPs and SLPs lend themselves well to a variety of structures including:

◆ all types of investment funds including vehicles to be used for carried interests or performance fees;

◆ asset holding structures;

◆ tax-transparent joint venture arrangements;

◆ family office holding structures; and

◆ structured finance transactions.

Test yourself 2.3

State four uses of a company incorporated in an offshore jurisdiction.

4. Trust company business services available offshore

Trust company business is a term that is used to describe the provision of:

◆ company administration services;

◆ trustee or fiduciary services;

◆ services to foundations.

The following are trust company business services that may be provided by a trust company in an offshore centre.

4.1 Acting as a company, a partnership or a foundation formation agent

In some offshore centres (for example, Jersey), companies may only be formed for non-residents by a person who is licensed to form companies under the law (e.g. a trust company). The trust company gives assurances to the registrar of companies that customer due diligence checks have been completed and that the companies do not (unless they have been specifically authorised to) undertake any 'sensitive' activities. Sensitive activities are those which may pose a risk to the regulators' need to protect the integrity of the jurisdiction or which may not be in the jurisdiction's best economic interests.

In some offshore centres, such as the British Virgin Islands, service providers make 'shelf' companies available. These are companies which have already been incorporated by the service provider and are therefore instantly available. The service provider, when approached for a shelf company, simply resigns themselves as directors of the company in favour of the person requesting a company and transfers any shares that they are holding. Jersey allows 'reserved companies' which are incorporated by service providers and the registry is advised that the company will be transferred to a client within the next six months, at which point the service provider must advise the registry of the identity of the beneficial owner.

4.2 Acting as, or arranging for another person to act as, a director or an alternate director of the company

Trust companies often provide individuals to act as directors to client entities. The individuals are usually directors or senior members of staff of the trust company.

In recent times, it has become common for the trust company or one of its wholly owned subsidiaries to be appointed as corporate directors of client entities. Individuals (or a committee of individuals) who are directors of the corporate director are then usually authorised to sign on behalf of the corporate director.

The appointment of a corporate director (as opposed to the appointment of individuals) has some administrative advantages. For example, there is increased flexibility as to which senior members of staff could sign documentation on behalf of a corporate director, whereas if individuals were appointed as directors, any documentation could not be signed if, for example, those members of staff were out of the office on business trips, were on annual leave or had left the employment of the organisation.

4.3 Acting as, or arranging for another person to act as, a secretary

In many jurisdictions, it is a requirement of the company's law that a company has a company secretary. It is not uncommon for the trust company or one of its wholly owned subsidiaries to be appointed as the company secretary. The company secretary often takes responsibility for signing important documentation on behalf of the company (e.g. its annual return or its tax return).

4.4 Acting as, or arranging for another person to act as, a shareholder or unit holder as nominee for another person

In some jurisdictions there is a requirement to notify the registrar of companies of the name and address of the company's shareholders upon incorporation and in some jurisdictions, on an annual basis. The identity of the shareholder becomes a matter of public record.

In offshore centres, it is extremely common for shares to be issued to the trust company business service provider who then becomes the legal shareholder. The trust company then signs a short private document (referred to as a declaration of trust) within which they admit and declare that they are holding the shares for the beneficial owner absolutely. The beneficial owner could be the client or the trustee of an overlying trust. In these circumstances, the trust company is referred to as a 'nominee shareholder'.

4.5 Acting as, or arranging for another person to act as, a trustee

Trust companies are very often appointed as the sole trustee of trusts which are settled by non-residents of the financial centre. The trust company itself is usually appointed as trustee although it is not uncommon for other wholly owned subsidiaries of the trust company to be appointed as trustees. It is common for a trust company to have a trust administration committee whose terms of reference provide for any two individual directors of the trust company to make decisions in relation to the day-to-day administration of trusts and companies that are under administration.

4.6 Acting as, or arranging for another person to act as, a partner of a partnership

The services provided are similar to those described in section 4.2 of this chapter.

4.7 Acting as, or arranging for another person to act as, a member of a Council of a foundation

In some offshore centres the provision of a member of the Council of a foundation is a regulated activity which must therefore be provided by a licensed trust company business service provider.

4.8 Providing accommodation, correspondence or administrative address for a company, a partnership, a foundation or any other person

The provision of an accommodation address has become less common in recent years. Historically, trust companies would forward mail to clients or keep it for them to collect. Developments in AML legislation and concerns over tax evasion have caused trust companies in well-regulated offshore centres to cease the practice or seek to understand that there are legitimate business reasons to explain why the service is required.

4.9 Providing a registered office or business address for a company, a partnership or foundation

It is a requirement of the company's law that every company has a **registered office** address which is notified to the authorities. The address notified to the registrar of companies (the equivalent of UK Companies House) is usually that of a trust company service provider.

registered office
The address of a company which has been notified to the authorities (as required by law) as the address to which legal notices can be sent.

Historically, the provision of a 'registered office only' service was seen as a low-risk service and was widely provided in offshore centres for a small fee. As the standard of regulation and awareness of money laundering and risk has increased, fewer trust companies are willing to provide this service alone, preferring to have full control over the entities under their administration.

The range of services provided has an impact on the level of information to which the trust company is privy. Trust companies may find themselves providing a registered office for companies that are involved in undesirable activities with connections to high-risk or unreputable jurisdictions. The regulators in well-administered jurisdictions expect trust companies to recognise the risks involved and to take steps to ensure that sufficient information about the company is held.

Many trust companies have ceased to provide registered office only services. Others have insisted that they are appointed as the secretary for such entities on the basis that they should be privy to additional information. In reality, however, if the directors are external, the trust company's appointment as secretary is unlikely to guarantee that they will receive additional information. In any case, the external directors could remove the secretary from its position at any time. Whenever a trust company provides limited services rather than the full range of trust company business services, there will be additional risks.

Making it work 2.1: Assa Limited

In December 2008, the US Department of the Treasury's Office of Foreign Assets Control (OFAC) reported that Assa Limited, a Jersey company whose registered office was provided by a local trust company was the parent organisation of Assa Corp, a shell company created and controlled by an Iranian government-owned bank, Bank Melli.

It was reported that Assa Limited co-owned a 36-storey skyscraper in New York with Assa Corp, a New York entity. It was alleged that the rental income from the office building was repeatedly transferred to Bank Melli through Assa Limited in violation of international sanctions to which Bank Melli was subject.

There were no reports that indicated that any service other than the provision of a registered office had been provided from within the Island of Jersey. This case highlights the huge risk for reputational damage that the provision of a registered office can present to an individual service provider and to an offshore centre.

5. Trust and company administration

5.1 The role of the trust and company administrator

It is not generally the role of the trust and company administrator to provide tax or legal advice to clients. Instead, the trust administrator may liaise with other professional advisers such as tax or legal advisers or accountants. Trust companies will strive to build good relationships with such intermediaries in order that the client's affairs are managed to a high standard and because they are a good source of new business opportunities. As such, professionals will often assist their clients to choose offshore services providers.

Many individuals who work in the trust and company administration sector belong to a professional body such as the Institute of Chartered Secretaries and Administrators (ICSA) or the Society for Trust and Estate Practitioners (STEP).

The demand for professionals to be members of such bodies in some offshore centres is driven by Codes of Practice issued by the regulator which impose a requirement for trust companies to have minimum levels of qualified staff. For example, in Jersey, 75% of staff who are decision makers must have attained a relevant qualification at diploma level or higher.

Trustees and directors both have fiduciary duties. It is important that administrators bear these duties in mind when administering offshore entities. A trustee must always act in the best interest of the trust (and similarly directors must act in the best interest of the company). A trust and company administrator should be familiar with the legislation governing trusts and companies and other entities in their jurisdiction.

Administrators should ensure that their actions are in accordance with the constitutional documentation concerning the entities under their administration – for example, the trust deed and any supplemental deeds relating to the trust and any memorandum and articles of a company.

An administrator should ensure that advice (for example, tax or legal advice) is sought where necessary. It is equally important that where advice has been obtained, it is appropriate (i.e. it covers all of the relevant circumstances) and that the entity is administered in accordance with the advice.

At times, policies and procedures can appear to delay or complicate needlessly the provision of services to clients. The policies and procedures of an organisation usually exist to protect the organisation or its employees against a risk that more junior employees may not understand. For this reason, they should always be followed. The organisation may be required to maintain some procedures (for example, those covering AML/CFT) by law. Others may exist in order to ensure that the trust company does not act outside of the scope of its licence to conduct financial services business. An administrator who seeks to understand the reason for the existence of such policies and procedures will enhance their technical knowledge and will be in a position to add value to their organisation by giving feedback to management on the effectiveness and efficiency of its policies and procedures.

Knowing the client is a key part of trust and company administration, and administrators will often be required to ask clients for customer due diligence information and should be in a position to explain the requirements of their organisation to the clients. This information should be considered and updated throughout the business relationship so that administrators are in a position to understand any transaction that they are involved with. This will allow the administrator to identify both the opportunities and the risks involved.

Administrators should be able to manage their client's expectations and should understand that at times, they may not be able to fulfil their client's wishes (for example, where to do so would expose the trust company to an unacceptable level of risk).

A good standard of record keeping is essential in order to demonstrate compliance with the laws, orders and codes of the jurisdiction, and to ensure that the client records are as useful as possible to the organisation, allowing it to service the client better.

Administrators should seek to protect the reputation of their organisation, their industry and their jurisdiction, and must bear in mind their personal obligations under the AML legislation.

5.2 Administration

Some trust companies offer administration only services to entities that they do not own or control. The term 'administration' is not always defined in the legislation of offshore centres; however, it may involve:

◆ the preparation of minutes and written resolutions;

◆ being appointed as the authorised signatories to a bank account;

◆ bookkeeping;

◆ the preparation of accounts;

◆ the preparation of correspondence on behalf of entities under administration; and

◆ the preparation of bank reconciliations.

5.3 Company administration

Company administration usually involves the management and control of the company's assets in a manner which is in the best interests of the company (and therefore ultimately in the best interests of all of the shareholders).

A company administrator's tasks may include:

◆ the preparation and submission of company formation documentation to the registrar of companies. This may include making an application for the company name, preparing a statement of particulars detailing the identity of directors and the registered office, making an application for consent to issue shares, and preparing the memorandum and articles of the company;

◆ the preparation of statutory filings (e.g. annual returns) or the filing of special resolutions with the companies registry;

◆ the preparation of notices and draft minutes for ad-hoc meetings of the directors of the company or for meetings that are required by law – for example, the AGM;

◆ the preparation of documentation such as that required in order to waive an annual AGM;

◆ the maintenance of company statutory records – for example, the register of members and the register of directors and secretaries; and

◆ the preparation of other documentation such as share certificates and declarations of trust.

5.4 Trust administration

Trust administration involves the administration of the trust assets in a manner that is in the best interest of the beneficiaries. Duties may include:

◆ liaising with the client and legal advisers in order to prepare initial trust documentation such as the trust deed;

◆ making distributions to beneficiaries of the trust, either when due to life tenants or after the trustee has exercised a power of discretion. This could involve preparing the relevant minutes of the trustee meeting at which the distribution was approved, preparing the instruction to the bank and presenting these documents to those with the authority to sign on behalf of the trustee;

◆ making loans to beneficiaries and preparing any loan agreements, trustee minutes and the payment documentation;

◆ preparing documentation (such as deeds of addition or exclusion) when adding or removing beneficiaries to or from the trust;

◆ corresponding with beneficiaries or the settlor; and

◆ monitoring receipt of income due to the trust and ensuring that its liabilities are paid in a timely manner.

Test yourself 2.4

Outline the role of a trust and company administrator.

---

6. Offshore insurance services

A wide range of insurance services are available from offshore centres. Offshore insurance sectors include domestic insurance, international insurance and insurance intermediaries. International insurance includes captive insurance, commercial insurance or international life and employee benefits. Insurance businesses offer products such as After The Event (ATE) insurance, credit insurance, professional indemnity insurance, reinsurance and transformer cells and captive insurance companies.

Guernsey Finance, a joint industry and government initiative to promote the island's finance sector, claims that Guernsey is the leading captive domicile in Europe and number four in the world. It claims that 40% of the leading 100 companies on the LSE with a captive insurance company has this in Guernsey.

6.1 Captive insurance companies

A captive insurance company is a subsidiary company (one owned by the parent company) formed to insure or reinsure the risks of its parent and/or associated group companies. Large companies who may spend a great deal of money on insurance premiums or who require a special type of cover not generally available from conventional insurers may set up offshore captive insurance companies. A number of offshore centres promote the incorporation of captive insurance companies.

Captives are usually formed to provide alternative risk management solutions to that of the conventional insurance markets. Captive insurance companies generally retain a portion of the overall risk and reinsure the remainder. For example, a large public limited company (plc) that provides employees with permanent health insurance as a part of their remuneration package may set up an offshore captive insurance company into which it pays 'premiums'. Higher health risks would be underwritten and any claims would be paid out of this offshore subsidiary. The large plc may benefit from interest generated on the excess funds invested which would be taxed at a low or zero rate.

Advantages of offshore captive insurance companies include the following.

◆ Many offshore centres offer captive insurance companies. They can therefore offer a high level of expertise in dealing with captive insurance.

◆ In some cases, offshore centres offer a less bureaucratic supervisory insurance regime.

◆ Premiums charged by commercial insurers include amounts that cover their profit margin and overheads. A captive insurance company can therefore be more cost-effective.

◆ Captive insurance companies offer flexibility. For example, at times the captive insurance company can take advantage of low rates by reinsuring a relatively large proportion of its risks. The cost of low reinsurance allows a captive insurance company to build its reserve base. At other times the captive insurance company can retain a larger proportion of its risks, maintaining cover for its parent even when commercial insurance is too costly.

◆ Captive insurance companies can make the process of claiming less bureaucratic and faster than the process would be if a third party insurer was involved.

◆ When lower claims than expected are experienced, the excess of net premiums over claims is retained by the group.

◆ The timing of premium payments can be arranged to ensure a best fit with the group's cash flow plans.

◆ Captive insurance companies may be able to provide cover that is not otherwise available.

While captive insurance companies offer potential advantages, they may also present disadvantages. For example, the setting up of a captive insurance company involves a capital commitment of funds at the outset. The captive is exposed to claims arising and may make substantial losses. Risks should only be placed in a captive if a tolerable claims record is contemplated. An offshore captive insurance company involves the delegation by the parent company to the directors of the offshore insurance company. They will therefore need to satisfy themselves that the offshore company has qualified staff with sufficient expertise and recognition of exposure to risk.

7. Legal services available in offshore centres

Many offshore centres also offer legal services. The bodies responsible for promoting offshore centres will often state the number of first-tier law firms or multijurisdictional law firms which operate from within their location.

As a part of the legal services provided, law firms offshore are often licensed to conduct trust company business. Some do so for specific reasons only; for example, they may deal with the formation of a company in connection with a property purchase but otherwise do not provide trust company business services.

Trustees often seek advice in relation to structures that are multijurisdictional. It is unlikely that a trustee would be familiar with the laws of every jurisdiction and it is therefore wise for them to take legal advice in order to ensure that entities under their control do not break any foreign laws and that any additional requirements are considered – for example, exchange controls that may restrict the outflows of money when dealing with certain jurisdictions.

Law firms are often involved with estate planning. This planning involves ensuring that wealth is passed to a client's next generation or intended beneficiaries. A law firm would play a key part in ensuring that any structure implemented is sufficiently robust to ensure that only the intended beneficiaries benefit and that any persons who should not benefit would have difficulty challenging the arrangements that are established.

It is common for law firms to be consulted at the stage where trusts are established and they are often involved in the preparation of trust deeds. Law firms are also often consulted throughout the period – for example, when a deed of addition of beneficiary (or exclusion) is required, or when varying the terms of a trust.

Some law firms have franchise or licence arrangements with trust companies whereby they provide the trust company with template documentation on an annual basis and allow them to use it free of charge or for an annual fee. The trustee is more likely to contact the law firm that provided the documentation, should a future legal issue ever arise.

Law firms will often give advice in relation to complex structures and strategies, for example, when planning insurance strategies such as captive insurance companies, or when listing a company's shares on a stock exchange.

Law firms are often consulted in connection with the registration of assets such as ships, yachts, aircrafts and trademarks or other intellectual property.

It has become more common for law firms to provide briefings and free seminars and technical updates to the financial services industry which assists in keeping finance professionals up to date and promotes the services of the law firm.

8. Tax compliance and tax planning

As previously explained, it is not common for offshore trust companies to provide tax advice or tax planning services, although some do have in-house advisers. It is more common for tax advisers to be a stand-alone business or to form a part of a legal or accountancy firm.

A local tax-planning firm with international reach and with particular expertise of the onshore jurisdictions that has close links to the offshore centre is particularly useful to offshore service providers.

Offshore taxation services broadly fall into two categories: tax planning and tax compliance.

8.1 Tax planning

Tax planning as part of an organisation's overall business strategy involves the avoidance of tax risks and benefitting as much as possible from opportunities to minimise taxation liabilities, within legal boundaries.

Tax planning includes the review of the financial affairs of a person and is an essential element of any estate planning. Many of the trust company business products discussed in section 3 of this chapter may be used as a part of a person's tax planning arrangements.

Professional tax management involves the monitoring of each corporate transaction (e.g. mergers, acquisitions and the purchase of assets) and identifying the tax implications from an early stage.

Tax services for investment funds cover a wide range of activities such as advice on the initial structuring of funds and how to manage tax residence and permanent establishment issues, providing guidance on how to make tax-efficient investments into many different jurisdictions, advising on how to interpret and react to tax legislation from all over the world, preparing tax reporting for fund investors, obtaining clearances or ruling from tax authorities on behalf of funds, and handling any tax compliance obligations.

8.2 Tax compliance

Tax compliance involves the preparation of tax returns for individuals and entities or the provision of information to tax authorities. Some trust companies prefer a tax adviser to liaise with the tax authorities on their behalf. Tax compliance services offshore may involve assisting clients of service providers who are the subject of a tax investigation or assisting clients to take advantage of disclosure facilities such as the Liechtenstein disclosure facility.

Many offshore entities have no tax to pay from within the offshore centre as they are exempt or taxed at a zero rate. It is not always necessary in these cases to involve a tax adviser in the preparation of the local tax return, which may simply involve confirming that there are no locally resident beneficial owners or local assets or income (usually with the exception of local bank interest) connected with the entity.

Test yourself 2.6

State two ways in which legal services may be used within the offshore business environment.

9. Investment business services

The investment business sector offshore includes the management, administration and custody of both open- and closed-ended collective investment funds, discretionary and non-discretionary asset management. Stockbroking, the provision of investment advice and performance monitoring may also be provided from within offshore centres.

9.1 Fund management

Offshore centres have been popular locations for collective investment schemes for many years. They are also popular choices for many private funds for institutional and professional investors. Traditionally, funds have been established as either open-ended or closed-ended investment companies or as unit trusts.

Some offshore centres are known for their specialised private investment funds which have been designed for other expert investors.

Retail funds including unit trusts or open-ended investment companies start off with a pool of cash from a number of investors. A professional fund manager invests the pool of cash with the intention of providing a better return than the individuals could achieve if they were to make an investment themselves. The funds are invested in accordance with the fund's particular objectives. Units or shares in the funds are issued to the investors in proportion to the amount invested.

The fund manager's responsibilities include selecting, buying and selling investments, calculating the value of the fund (daily in many cases) and issuing units to new investors or buying units back at the unit prices.

The fund manager issues periodic reports to all unit holders, covering the fund's activities and current investments.

9.2 Portfolio management services

Private portfolios are managed for the benefit of one individual or entity. Many trusts and companies hold investment portfolios that are professionally managed by an investment manager.

Portfolio managers often specify a minimum sum that they are willing to manage on behalf of any particular person. Portfolio managers who provide services to clients of trust companies, for example, may allow lower minimum investments owing to the relationship that they have with the trust company.

Portfolio valuations and reports are produced for clients, usually on a quarterly basis, although for wealthy clients, a more personal service may be provided and, in these cases, reports may be produced on a more frequent basis.

There are three types of portfolio management services available. These include execution only, advisory management and discretionary management.

Execution only

Where an investor knows which security they want to purchase or sell, they may deal through a broker on an 'execution only' basis. Customers who deal on an execution only basis are not given any advice by the firm when they make investment decisions. The only responsibility of the firm is one of 'best execution', i.e. to implement the customer's investment decisions at the best price available.

Advisory management

Advisory customers are those to whom the firm gives advice and investment management services; however, investment decisions are always made by the customer.

Discretionary management

With this service, the customer empowers the investment manager to exercise discretion regarding the buying, retaining and selling of the investments in order to meet the client's objectives.

Offshore trustees or companies would most commonly appoint an investment manager on this basis as they may not necessarily have the skills to manage an investment portfolio themselves.

The appointment of an investment manager on a discretionary basis does not absolve trustees or directors of their duties to monitor the investments. It is common in offshore centres for corporate service providers to appoint independent consultants to review their investment portfolio performance upon receipt of portfolio valuations for a small fee. This offers some additional comfort that the portfolio is being managed properly.

Test yourself 2.7

Explain the three types of portfolio management services available.

Portfolio planning

The following is a non-exhaustive list of factors that should be considered when planning an investment portfolio:

◆ The client's attitude to risk.

◆ The tax efficiency of the investment portfolio.

◆ The client's family circumstances – for example, whether there is a dependent child or spouse to provide for.

◆ The accessibility of the investment. Some clients may need to be able to access the funds at relatively short notice or in the case of an emergency.

◆ Whether there are any income or capital growth requirements.

◆ Whether the portfolio will provide sufficient protection against inflation. For example, cash does not usually form a large part of an investment portfolio for significant periods of time.

◆ Whether there are any ethical investment requirements.

◆ The client's time horizons.

Asset allocation

Investment portfolios usually include an element of cash, fixed interest securities and equities. The proportion of the split between these elements will reflect economic factors and each client's circumstances and requirements. The investments will be across a range of jurisdictions and industries and possibly currencies. Investment managers should aim to achieve the maximum return possible, while taking as little risk as possible.

Cash

Cash forms an important part of any portfolio for the following reasons.

◆ It provides funds to meet expected expenditure (such as trustee fees).

◆ It provides funds to meet extraordinary expenses.

◆ It can provide a shelter during times of significant volatility.

◆ It provides a fund that can be used to take advantage of market opportunities as they arise.

Fixed interest

As the name suggests, fixed interest securities pay a fixed amount of income. When interest rates go up, the capital value of fixed interest rate securities falls. Fixed interest securities usually provide a higher rate of return than cash.

Equities

Equities are the most volatile elements of the portfolio; however, they also provide the greatest potential for capital growth over the long term. In order to reduce risk, the equities are usually spread over a range of geographic locations and industries, providing diversification.

Chapter summary

◆ The offshore financial services sector typically offers trust company business services, insurances services, investment management services, legal services and tax planning and compliance services.

◆ Trust company business products that are available offshore include trusts, companies, foundations and partnerships.

◆ Trust company business services that are often provided include acting as a company or partnership formation agent, acting as a director, secretary or nominee shareholder, acting as a trustee or partner or a member of a foundation Council and providing a registered office or administrative address to a company, partnership or foundation.

◆ Whenever a trust company provides limited services, such as providing a registered office only, it will face additional risks.

◆ The role of a trust and company administrator is varied and includes a wide range of duties which should be carried out in the best interest of the company or beneficiaries, having regard at all times to the constitution of the relevant entities under administration, their objectives and all applicable laws of the jurisdiction.

◆ Offshore insurance services sectors usually offer a wide range of insurance products such as ATE insurance, reinsurance and captive insurance companies. Captive insurance companies provide alternative risk management solutions to those of the conventional insurance markets.

◆ Legal services offshore include the provision of legal advice in connection with simple and complex structures, perhaps as a part of a person's estate planning (involving Trust Company Business products) when planning insurance strategies such as captive insurance companies or when listing a company's shares on a stock exchange.

◆ Offshore taxation services broadly fall into two categories: tax planning and tax compliance. Tax planning involves the planning surrounding the avoidance of tax risks and the benefitting as much as possible from tax opportunities to minimise taxation liability.

◆ Investment management services offshore include fund management – for example, in relation to collective investment schemes, private portfolio management services on an execution only, an advisory management or a discretionary management basis. Portfolio planning involves the consideration of a number of factors about the investor (such as their attitude to risk, family circumstances, the taxation consequences, the accessibility of the investments of any capital or income requirements). Portfolios usually contain an element of cash, fixed interest and equities.

Part Two

The legal environment

After studying this part, students will gain an understanding of the importance of English law in offshore jurisdictions and will understand the difference between common law jurisdictions, which recognise the distinction between legal and equitable rights, and civil law jurisdictions, which tend not to. This part explains the relationship between common law and equity. Students will be able to discuss the advantages and disadvantages of legislation, and the rules and issues surrounding statutory interpretation. Similarly, students will be able to discuss the advantages and disadvantages of the doctrine of judicial precedent under which the courts are obliged to stand by their earlier decisions. Students will gain an understanding of the essential elements required in order to form a binding contract (agreement constituted by an offer and acceptance, consideration, legal intentions, capacity and legality) and identify when there has been a breach of contract and the consequences of such breach. Students will be able to describe the common law remedy of damages and the equitable remedies that may be awarded by the courts.

Learning outcomes

At the end of this part, students will be able to:

- discuss the importance of English law in offshore jurisdictions;
- explain the development of English law;
- discuss the features of the common law system and the system of equity;
- distinguish between civil law and common law jurisdictions;
- understand the distinction between legal and equitable rights;
- explain the relationship between common law and equity;
- explain the advantages and disadvantages of statute law;
- discuss statutory interpretation;
- explain case law and the doctrine of binding precedent;
- discuss the advantages and disadvantages of case law;
- define a contract and explain the essentials required to form a contract;
- define offer, acceptance, an invitation to treat and consideration;
- outline contractual capacity;
- outline circumstances surrounding intention to create legal relations;
- describe situations of termination of an offer; and
- discuss breach of conditions and the remedies available.

Chapter three
The importance of English law

List of topics

1. The importance of English law in offshore jurisdictions
2. The development of English law
3. The distinction between civil law and common law jurisdictions
4. Legislation
5. Case law

Introduction

This chapter outlines the reason that English laws are of major significance in many offshore centres. The two historical sources of law, **common law** and **equity**, are discussed. The chapter explains how the common law is embodied in judicial decisions as, under the system, the judges are guided by previous decisions of the courts. The chapter also outlines the system of equity (administered by the Court of Chancery) that developed alongside the common law in an effort to introduce fairness where justice was not done under the common law system. The chapter outlines the relationship between common law and equity, and gives a brief outline of statutory law. The rules of statutory interpretation are discussed, as are the advantages and limitations of both legislation and case law.

common law
A system of law under which the judges are guided by previous decisions of the courts under the doctrine of judicial precedent.

equity
A system of law administered by the Court of Chancery that developed alongside the common law where justice could not be done.

1. The importance of English law in offshore jurisdictions

English law is of major significance to offshore practitioners. Many offshore centres have legal systems based on principles of English law (which applies to England and Wales only, and is distinct from Scots law). For example, the Crown Dependencies have their own legal system and jurisprudence; however, their statutory provisions are often modelled on English law and, where this is the case, English cases are frequently referenced by their courts. The significance of this will become clear after you are familiar with the concept of judicial precedent (discussed in section 5.1 of this chapter). In addition, laws passed in the Crown Dependencies require royal assent from the UK's Privy Council.

Although local laws in many offshore centres have been developed in order to accommodate requirements that are specific to the jurisdiction, these are often largely based upon similar English laws. This is especially the case where the offshore centre has a close relationship with England. They may differ in areas such as direct taxation, company law and financial supervision.

Many laws that are applicable in England are applicable by extension in overseas territories (such as the British Virgin Islands) and in many independent Commonwealth countries including many offshore centres.

1.1 The Judicial Committee of the Privy Council

When the British Empire became the Commonwealth of Nations, many member countries chose to retain their legal links with the UK. The Judicial Committee still hears 'appeals to Her Majesty in Council' from many countries worldwide in respect of every kind of case (including civil and criminal cases).

The Judicial Committee of the Privy Council is the highest (and final) court of appeal for many current and former Commonwealth countries, as well as the UK's overseas territories, Crown Dependencies and military sovereign base areas. Should the Privy Council choose to do so, it may reverse the decision of the lower court in the country from which the case was referred.

Case law 3.1: Spread Trustee Company Limited v. Sarah Ann Acato Hutcheson and others

On 15 June 2011, the Judicial Committee of the Privy Council delivered its judgement in relation to an appeal following a decision of the Court of Appeal of Guernsey on 26 November 2009 in relation to the case known as Spread Trustee Company Limited v. Sarah Ann Acato Hutcheson and others [2011].

The Trustee held that the liability of a trustee for gross negligence could lawfully be excluded as a matter of Guernsey customary law and under the 1989 Law. The issue raised by the appeal was whether it was permissible for a trust deed to exclude a trustee's liability for gross negligence prior to the entry into force of the Trusts (Amendment) (Guernsey) Law 1990 (the Amendment Law), which expressly prohibited such an exclusion.

The trust deed contained a clause which stated: 'In the execution of the trusts and powers hereof no trustee shall be liable for any loss to the Trust Fund arising in consequence of the failure depreciation or loss of any investments made in good faith or by reason of any mistake or omission made in good faith or of any other matter or thing except wilful and individual fraud and wrongdoing on the part of the trustee who is sought to be made liable.'

The Board of the Judicial Committee of the Privy Council allowed the appeal by a majority of 3:2. Within the judgement it was stated that 'there is no reason to treat Guernsey law as following the Scottish view on this point in preference to the view taken under English law with which the Guernsey law of trusts is more closely associated'.

This case demonstrates the importance of English law to offshore centres and is an example of the Privy Council overturning the decisions of lower courts.

The full judgement can be found on the website of the Privy Council at www.jcpc.gov.uk

2. The development of English law

The two historical sources of law are common law and equity.

2.1 The common law

The earliest element of the legal system to develop was the common law applied by royal courts. Under the common law system, the English courts were guided by and obliged to follow the decisions that had been made in earlier cases. The common law is therefore embodied in judicial decisions and over the years has become a comprehensive set of rules. The concept of the court being guided by its own previous decisions is known as the concept of judicial precedent (see section 5.1 below).

Each time the court applies an established principle to new facts, the common law develops. Similarly, it develops in circumstances where the courts choose not to apply such a principle.

While the common law provided some certainty and consistency in relation to the outcomes of future cases, there were some disadvantages of the system. Strict adherence to the doctrine of precedent under the common law system resulted in a rigid and inflexible set of rules which, when applied, did not always amount to justice being done. Much emphasis was placed on procedure which meant that a claimant might lose their case because of a minor technicality of wording. In addition, where a case was won, only a limited remedy of damages was available under the common law and this did not always result in a fair resolution.

2.2 Equity

Equity was developed several hundred years after common law as a system of law applied by the Court of Chancery. Where justice did not appear to be done under common law principles, an otherwise innocent party who could not obtain redress for grievances could apply to the King, who had unfettered, unlimited powers to intervene to determine cases on an ad-hoc basis in order to achieve a fair result. The King later delegated his power to the Chancellor, who became the head of the Court of Chancery.

The Court of Chancery sought to decide cases in accordance with what was right, just and fair rather than adhering to the letter of the law. Unlike the common law, the new system of law (referred to as 'equity') did not focus on procedural technicalities but rather focussed on achieving a just result supplementing the common law and introducing the concept of fairness. This system developed into a whole system of law, with a specific set of legal principles and rules.

A system of common law, based on strict rules, and a system of equity, based on fair dealings between parties, therefore developed in parallel.

Test yourself 3.1

How does common law differ from equity?

2.3 The distinction between legal and equitable rights

The concept of the trust is said to have arisen from the Court of Chancery as a result of the unfairness of the common law systems during the time of the Crusades in the 12th and 13th century in England. Land owners who had entrusted their property to others to look after while they went to fight in the Crusades often returned to find that they could not insist that their property be conveyed back to them. The Crusaders petitioned the king (and later the Chancellor) to intervene. The Chancellor recognised that each Crusader was the true owner and ordered the legal owner to convey the property back to the Crusader. Over time the recognition that the legal owner of property was not necessarily the person who was entitled to benefit from it (i.e. that there is a distinction between the legal and equitable rights) developed into the concept of the trust that is widely accepted in the common law jurisdictions today. This is that while the legal ownership of the trust property lies with the trustee, the equitable (beneficial) ownership lies with the beneficiaries.

The relationship between common law and equity
Where it applies, the common law applies automatically. The court, however, has discretion to apply the rules of equity and to grant an equitable remedy if it chooses to do so.

Equity and common law often conflicted. In a landmark case known as the Earl of Oxford's case, 1615, it was decided that where common law and equity conflict, equity must prevail. In the UK, the Senior Courts Act 1981 also provides that 'every court exercising jurisdiction in England or Wales in any civil case or matter shall continue to administer law and equity on the basis that, wherever there is any conflict or variance between the rules of equity and the rules of the common law with reference to the same matter, the rules of equity shall prevail'.

3. The distinction between civil law and common law jurisdictions

Offshore jurisdictions can either be civil law jurisdictions or common law jurisdictions. Countries of the former British Commonwealth usually have common law systems. Offshore centres such as the Bahamas and Bermuda are considered to be 'common law jurisdictions'.

The civil law jurisdictions generally have a system of law which has been developed from and is based on Roman law. Civil law principles are found in countries such as those in continental Europe. There are many offshore centres that have laws based on civil law principles such as Liechtenstein, Luxembourg and Switzerland.

The civil law system is a codified system in which laws are comprehensively set out in detail in a statutory code. The judges in the courts that implement the law regard the code only and need not regard the outcome of previous cases as the **doctrine of judicial precedent** does not form a part of the system.

Trusts are mostly administered in common law jurisdictions where there is certainty about their recognition and the way that they are treated in law. The law in such jurisdictions will allow for their creation and the provisions of the trust will be recognised and enforced by the courts of those jurisdictions.

The laws of civil law jurisdictions do not generally recognise the division between legal and equitable ownership and it is usually therefore not possible to create a trust in such jurisdictions. The concept of a trust is thus not understood in civil law jurisdictions and it does not always appeal to clients who have dealings with such jurisdictions.

Some civil law jurisdictions have endeavoured to make it more attractive to administer trusts from within their jurisdiction. Switzerland, for example, is a civil law jurisdiction which does not have its own trusts law. However, in July 2007, it ratified the Hague Convention on the law applicable to trusts and their recognition, which means that it now recognises their existence and it also made changes to some of its laws in an attempt to reduce the uncertainty of the legal environment surrounding the administration of trusts. Common law jurisdictions have increased their offerings of products such as foundations as an alternative to trusts, as these are better known to clients who are more familiar with civil law.

Some jurisdictions have hybrid systems of law in that they follow a mixed law tradition (Liechtenstein and Panama).

doctrine of judicial precedent
Under the doctrine of judicial precedent, the judge is bound to follow decisions that have been reached in earlier court cases.

Test yourself 3.2

How does the law in common law jurisdictions differ from that of civil law jurisdictions?

4. Legislation

Statutory laws are enacted by the government or other authorised bodies (i.e. legislatures) through the process of legislation. In the UK, primary legislation is made by Parliament.

Legislation, however, may also be made by other bodies under authority of primary legislation – for example, when secondary legislation is enacted. Secondary legislation may be referred to as regulations. When enacting laws in the UK, Parliament must have regard to obligations that arise as a result of being a part of the European Union.

4.1 Advantages of legislation

◆ Any issue can be addressed by statute law at any time by Parliament.
◆ Statute is carefully constructed and is subject to a process of scrutiny which should ensure that it achieves the result desired by the law makers.
◆ Statute law is available to and accessible to the general public (which is an advantage over case law, which is difficult to establish and not found in one place).

4.2 Disadvantages of legislation

◆ Statutes are numerous and voluminous.
◆ Statute law cannot anticipate all circumstances or situations which may arise.
◆ Parliament has limited time to consider the draft legislation.
◆ Statute law is inflexible.
◆ Governments sometimes lack the resources (including time and finances) to amend legislation when it becomes out of date and no longer fit for purpose.
◆ Statute can take a long time to change, due to the process involved.
◆ The public can be apathetic about the legislation process.
◆ Interpretation of statute is often required.

4.3 Statutory interpretation

The effectiveness of any statute depends to some extent on the interpretation given to it by the courts, especially where the wording of the statute is ambiguous. In interpreting the words of a statute, the courts have developed a number of basic principles of statutory interpretation which, although referred to as rules, are instead different approaches to statutory interpretation. These general principles are not found in any statute as they have developed from the decisions of the courts. The principles are referred to as the literal rule, the golden rule, the mischief rule and the contextual rule. There is no established order of application where the general principles conflict.

The literal rule

The literal rule places emphasises on the literal (i.e. it relies on the plain and ordinary) meaning of the words contained within statutory provisions. Its advantage is that it respects Parliament as the supreme law maker.

However, the rule has been criticised. In a 1969 report, the Law Commission criticised the literal rule for the following reasons.

◆   It does not give due weight to the wider context of the law maker.

◆   Where the literal rule is followed, it is possible that legislation writers do not take into account the facts or circumstances that judges later consider.

◆   Law draftsmen do not always choose words to describe the situations intended to be covered by the provision.

◆   To use the literal rule means to allow no room for difference of opinion.

The golden rule

Under the golden rule, where the literal meaning of the statute would lead to an absurd result that is unlikely to have been the intention of the law draftsmen, the judge can depart from the literal meaning – for example, R v. Allen (1872).

The mischief rule

The mischief rule seeks to ensure that statute should be interpreted with regard to the true intent of its makers. The rule was established in the Landmark case known as Heydon's Case (1584). The court set out that for the sure and true interpretation of all statutes, judges should consider three factors:

1.   what was the law before the act was passed;

2.   what problem, or mischief was the act trying to remedy; and

3.   what remedy was Parliament trying to provide.

The judge should then interpret the act in such a way as to deal with the problem that Parliament was trying to address.

The case concluded that having considered those things, the office of the judges is always to make such construction as shall suppress the mischief and advance the remedy.

The mischief rule was considered by the Law Commission to be a more satisfactory approach to statutory interpretation than the literal rule, as it requires a judge to interpret the legislation in a manner which promotes the general aims or purposes of the legislation. This is influenced by the European approach to statutory interpretation which focuses on giving effect to the purpose behind the legislation; in the words of Lord Denning, 'looking to the spirit of the law rather than the letter of the law.'

The contextual rule

The contextual rule is that words should be interpreted in context. This means that the purpose of the statute should be considered when interpreting words within it.

Test yourself 3.3

What is the literal rule of statutory interpretation?

5. Case law

As explained in section 2.1 of this chapter, the English courts were guided by and obliged to follow the decisions that had been reached in earlier court cases. These judicial decisions, over the years, have become a comprehensive set of rules referred to as 'case law'. Each time the court applies an established principle to new facts or chooses not to apply an established principle, case law develops.

5.1 The doctrine of judicial precedent

The doctrine of judicial precedent (or binding precedent) means that the judge is bound to apply an existing precedent (e.g. a previous court decision) from an earlier case to the facts of the case before them, provided that there are no material differences between the cases and providing of course that there are adequate and reliable reports of earlier decisions.

stare decisis
A Latin term for 'let the decision stand'.

The doctrine of judicial precedent is often expressed in the maxim **stare decisis**, which is Latin for 'let the decision stand', although there are instances where a precedent will not be binding on future courts. For example, if the facts of the case are materially different, the court may distinguish the earlier case on the facts and thereby avoid following it as a precedent. In addition, a statute could be passed at any time and therefore a conflicting precedent would not be followed after its introduction.

ratio decidendi
The *ratio decidendi* of a case is any rule of law or legal principle that is treated by the judge as necessary for the basis of the decision made.

Only the **ratio decidendi** of a case is binding on future decisions; other precedents may be merely persuasive. Whether a court is bound by a particular precedent depends on its position in the hierarchy of courts. Generally, the decisions of superior courts are binding on lower courts and the decisions of lower courts are not binding on higher courts.

5.2 Ratio decidendi

The *ratio decidendi* (the reasoning behind the decision) of a case is any rule of law or legal principle that is treated by the judge as necessary for the basis of the decision made or is a necessary part of the judge's direction to the jury.

obiter dicta
The *obiter dicta* of a case are words that are said 'by the way' and do not form a part of the *ratio decidendi*.

The **obiter dicta** of a case are words that are said 'by the way'. The *obiter dicta* do not form a part of the *ratio decidendi*. Only the *ratio decidendi* is binding on future cases; however, the *obiter dicta* may be treated as having persuasive authority in future cases. Persuasive precedents are those that are not binding in future cases; however, judges in later cases may be influenced by them.

Test yourself 3.4

What is the *ratio decidendi* of a case?

5.3 The advantages of precedent

◆ Precedents should provide consistency and this leads to certainty about the way that the law will be decided.

◆ Precedents should ensure that the law is decided fairly.

◆ Precedents are tested (i.e. based on actual cases) whereas legislation is often untested.

◆ As precedents can be avoided, they are adaptable to new situations and are therefore more flexible than legislation.

◆ As precedents are based on facts, they are practical in nature, unlike legislation.

5.4 The disadvantages of precedent

◆ Judges can be forced to make distinctions that are not logical in order to avoid an unfair result.

◆ Judges may distinguish on facts in order to avoid a precedent which leads to uncertainty about the way that the law will be decided.

◆ The discretion of the judge is limited.

◆ It may take some time for a point of law to be tested (it will only be tested as and when a case arises).

◆ Judges may be unable to avoid deciding in line with a precedent which produces an unfair result.

◆ It can be difficult to establish which facts are the *ratio decidendi* (and therefore the binding elements) of a case.

◆ Unlike legislation, cases are not easily located and they are numerous.

Chapter summary

◆ English law is of major significance to offshore practitioners as many offshore centres have legal systems based on principles of English law. In addition, the Judicial Committee of the Privy Council is the highest court of appeal in many offshore centres in current and former commonwealth countries.

◆ There are two historical sources of law: the common law and equity.

◆ The common law system is embodied in judicial decisions as, under the system, the courts are obliged to follow the decisions that have been made in earlier cases in accordance with the concept of judicial precedent.

◆ The doctrine of judicial precedent is often expressed as the maxim *stare decisis*, which is Latin for 'let the decision stand'. Under the doctrine of judicial precedent, the court is obliged to follow the decisions made in earlier cases. Only the *ratio decidendi* (the reason behind the decision) is binding on future decisions; other precedents may be merely persuasive. The court is not obliged to follow decisions of lower courts.

◆ Equity (applied by the Court of Chancery) developed in parallel with common law as a result of justice not being done under the common law. The focus of equity is on fairness and what is right and just, rather than adhering to the letter of the law and focussing on procedural technicalities.

◆ The concept of the trust is said to have arisen out of equity as the Court of Chancery recognised the distinction between legal and equitable ownership of property.

◆ The common law applies automatically; however, the court has discretion to apply the rules of equity and to grant an equitable remedy (instead of the limited remedy of damages available under common law) if it chooses to do so.

◆ Where equity and common law conflicts, equity must prevail.

◆ Civil law jurisdictions differ from common law systems as they have developed from and are based on Roman law. Civil law is a codified system. The concept of a trust is less understood in civil law jurisdictions.

◆ Statutory laws are enacted by the government or other authorised bodies through the process of legislation. It often requires interpretation. The main rules of statutory interpretation are the literal rule, the golden rule and the mischief rule.

Chapter four
Contract law

List of topics

1. Contract law
2. The essentials required to form a contract
3. Performance
4. Breach of conditions
5. Remedies for breach of contract

Introduction

This chapter outlines the essentials required in order to form a valid (legally binding) contract. The essential elements of agreement (offer and acceptance), consideration and intention to create legal relations and capacity are explained. The chapter discusses what constitutes performance of a contract and outlines what constitutes a breach of contract; it finally explains the remedies for breach of contract including the common law remedy of damages and the equitable remedies such as specific performance, injunction, Mareva injunction and rescission.

1. Contract law

In order to gain a basic understanding of contract law, this chapter discusses the law of England and Wales.

Some offshore centres have based their contract law on that of England and Wales, although the extent to which they do so varies from jurisdiction to jurisdiction. Jersey, for example, follows English law for much of its law; however, in the case of contract law, it has referred to both Norman Law (French) cases and English cases. The Jersey Law Commission issued a consultation paper in 2002 entitled 'the Jersey law of contract' which sets out some of the difficulties that doing so has presented to the jurisdiction in terms of certainty about the way that the law is applied.

2. The essentials required to form a contract

A valid contract is an agreement between parties that is made with the intention for it to be legally binding and supported by **consideration**. A contract can be made in any form. It may be made orally, in writing or may be inferred from the conduct of the parties to it. The law requires that some contracts (e.g. those involving the sale of land) must be made in writing. In the offshore professional environment, it is unlikely that administrators would deal with oral contracts and therefore contracts will instead be made in writing. The essential elements are:

consideration
Consideration must be given by both parties to a contract and is defined as 'some right, interest, profit or benefit accruing to one party, or some forbearance, detriment, loss or responsibility given, suffered or undertaken by the other' (Currie v. Misa).

◆ agreement (made by an offer and acceptance);

◆ consideration; and

◆ intention to create legal relations.

In addition, for the contract to be enforceable, the parties to it must have legal capacity to contract and the contract must not be illegal.

In the case of Carlill v. Carbolic Smoke Ball Co (1893), the advertisement for a medicinal smoke ball advertised that '£100 reward will be paid by the Carbolic Smoke Ball Company to any person who contracts the influenza after having used the ball three times daily for two weeks according to the printed directions supplied with each ball'. Mrs Carlill used the smoke ball in accordance with the instructions and claimed the £100 after contracting influenza. The Smoke Ball company refused to pay the money arguing that no legally binding contract had come into being.

The case illustrated the following points in relation to contract law.

◆ All of the essential elements of a contract were present.

◆ The advertisement constituted an offer. The offer was made to 'anybody who performed the conditions named in the advertisement'. Offers do not therefore need to be made to a named individual and can be made to 'the whole of the world'.

◆ Acceptance of the offer was performance of the condition (i.e. taking the medication in accordance with the printed directions).

◆ Acceptance was communicated, albeit after the performance of the condition.

◆ The taking of the medication as per the printed directions was deemed to be adequate consideration.

◆ It was established that the wording of the advertisement was a definite legal promise that it intended to be acted upon (i.e. intention to create legal relations was present).

Test yourself 4.1

What are the essential elements of a valid contract?

2.1 The offer

An offer is a definite expression of willingness to be bound on specific terms without further negotiations. An offer cannot be vague or uncertain and there must be a clear intention to be bound by the terms of the contract.

An offer can be in any form (i.e. written, oral or by conduct) and must be communicated to the offeree and must be open at the time when it is accepted. An offer may be made to an individual or open to a number of individuals. The famous case of Carlill v. Carbolic Smoke Ball Co (1893) (discussed in section 2 of this chapter) illustrates this particular point.

An offer must be distinguished from the mere supply of information which is not intended to be acted upon and instead is intended to enlighten the other party. An **invitation to treat** is not an offer.

invitation to treat
An invitation to another person to make an offer.

Invitation to treat

An invitation to treat is distinct from a binding offer to be bound. An invitation to treat is not an offer but an invitation to someone else to make an offer. An invitation to treat cannot therefore be 'accepted' to form a contract. A person who invites another to make an offer is entitled to change their mind.

The general rule is that advertisements are invitations to treat rather than offers. However, in Carlill v. Carbolic Smoke Ball Co (1893), the wording of the advertisement was such that it was considered to be an offer that could be accepted without further negotiation.

The display of goods on a shop shelf is considered to be an invitation to treat rather than an offer. This is demonstrated by the case of Pharmaceutical Society of Great Britain v. Boots Cash Chemists (1953). In this case, the law stated that the sale of certain pharmaceuticals must be dealt with under the supervision of a qualified pharmacist. The pharmaceuticals subject to the law were displayed on the Boots shop shelf with a price tag and the arrangement was that customers paid for the goods at the till where a qualified pharmacist was present. The Pharmaceutical Society claimed that the display of goods in such a manner was contrary to the law, as the sale took place when the customer placed the goods in the basket, which was not supervised by a pharmacist. The court held that the display of goods in a shop was an invitation to treat and not an offer. In such situations it was the customer who made the offer and the shop worker could accept or reject this at the till where the pharmacist was present.

The advertisement of a selling price in response to a request for information is not an offer.

Stop and think 4.1

Is an advertisement that states 'Car for sale – good condition – £1,000' an invitation to treat or an offer?

Acceptance of an offer

Acceptance of an offer is an unconditional agreement to all of the terms of the offer, although acceptance in contracts may be 'subject to contract'. Acceptance may be oral or written, or may be inferred by conduct unless otherwise specified in the terms of the contract.

The general rule is that acceptance must be communicated to the offeror to be effective; however, the case of Carlill v. Carbolic Smoke Ball Co (1893) demonstrated that there are situations where the offer dispenses with this requirement. It is possible for acceptance of an offer to be implied from conduct as illustrated in the case of Carlill where the use of the smoke ball amounted to acceptance.

If an offer is revoked before it is accepted, the offer is considered to have been terminated.

Termination of an offer

revocation
An offer may terminated by revocation. This means that the offeror cancels the offer and it is no longer open for acceptance.

An offer can be terminated by **revocation** (which must be communicated to the offeree), by rejection (which could be an outright rejection of the offer or by the making of a counter offer) or because it has lapsed. An offer could lapse on the death of either party or after the expiry of a period of time specified within the contract or after a reasonable amount of time.

2.2 Consideration

Consideration was defined in Currie v. Misa (1875) as being 'some right, interest, profit or benefit accruing to one party, or some forbearance, detriment, loss or responsibility given, suffered or undertaken by the other'. All contracts must be supported by some form of consideration from each party (unless they are made by deed). Consideration is the price paid for the promise. English law does not enforce a bare promise; it will only enforce a bargain. This means that each party to the contract must promise to give or do something for the other. This element of exchange is called consideration.

In the case of Carlill v. Carbolic Smoke Ball Co (1893), the consideration was the taking of the medication as per the printed direction. Consideration could include the making of a payment or the provision of a service.

The following is true of consideration.

◆ Consideration must be provided by both parties to contract before it is likely to be binding.

◆ Consideration need not be adequate, but must be sufficient.

◆ Past consideration is not sufficient consideration and is therefore not valid.

◆ Performance of existing duties is not sufficient consideration.

◆ Illegal acts do not amount to sufficient consideration.

Case law 4.1: Chappell & Co Ltd v. Nestle Co Ltd

The point that consideration need not be adequate but must be sufficient is illustrated in the case Chappell & Co Ltd v. Nestle Co Ltd (1960). Nestle had promised to give away a copy of a record to people who sent in three chocolate bar wrappers and a postal order for 1s 6d. A royalty needed to be paid on the ordinary retail selling price to Chappell & Co, which owned the copyright. Nestle said 1s 6d was the ordinary retail selling price; however, Chappell & Co disagreed. As the wrappers were worthless to Nestle when they received them, it was argued that they could not amount to consideration. The judge thought this irrelevant and overturned a previous court decision. The judge commented that a contracting party can stipulate for what consideration they choose and argued that 'a peppercorn does not cease to be good consideration if it is established that the promisee does not like pepper and will throw away the corn'.

Case law 4.2: Stilk v. Myrick

In the case of Stilk v. Myrick (1809), Stilk agreed to be paid wages of £5 a month prior to beginning a voyage from London to the Baltic and back as a seaman. During the voyage, two men deserted. Myrick, the captain, entered into an agreement with the remaining crew, that they should have the wages of those who had deserted if he could not procure two other workers. No other workers joined the crew; however, Myrick later refused to pay the extra wages. It was held that Myrick's promise was not enforceable due to the consideration Stilk had provided for it – the performance of a duty he already owed to Myrick under contract. Performance of existing duties was not good consideration for Myrick's promise to increase his wages.

2.3 Legal intentions

The parties to a contract must have had an intention that the arrangement would be legally binding (i.e. that they would enter into a legal relationship). Legal intention need not be explicit or in writing, and may be implied from the circumstances.

The following assumptions are generally held by the courts.

◆ Social, domestic and family arrangements are not usually intended to be binding.

◆ Commercial arrangements are usually intended to be binding.

Case law 4.3: Balfour v. Balfour (1919)

In the case of Balfour v. Balfour (1919), Mr and Mrs Balfour had visited England when Mrs Balfour became ill. Mr Balfour agreed to pay his wife maintenance each month until she could return home with him; however, he later asked to remain separated from her. It was held that social relationships are presumed unenforceable, because people do not generally intend social promises to create legal consequences.

Contracts that are signed under duress are considered to be void (i.e. not legally binding) from the outset and are not therefore enforceable.

2.4 Capacity

capacity
A party to a contract must have legal capacity (the power legally to enter into it) for it to be enforceable. Vulnerable people such as children do not have capacity.

For a contract to be binding, the parties to it must have a legal **capacity** to enter into it. That is to say, they must have the power legally to enter into the contract. As a matter of public policy, vulnerable individuals are protected by various pieces of legislation. In the UK, contracts made by minors (those who have not reached the age of 18 years) are usually voidable and contracts made with people who are mentally incapacitated are not enforceable.

It is therefore vital that offshore practitioners ensure that where a contract is entered into with third parties, those third parties have legal capacity to contract, otherwise the contract may not be enforceable.

2.5 Legality

Contracts that are deemed to be illegal cannot be enforced.

3. Performance

The general rule is that contracts must be completely performed.

Case law 4.4: Cutter v. Powell (1795)

quantum meruit
This term means 'as much as he deserved'.

In Cutter v. Powell (1795), Cutter had contracted to work on a ship during a voyage; however, he did not survive the voyage. As he had worked for part of the contract, his widow argued that she was entitled to a *quantum meruit* award (meaning 'as much as he has deserved') in relation to the work that her husband had performed. It was held that the instrument was an entire contract, under which he had failed to meet his obligations. No compensation for part performance was therefore paid.

There are some exceptions to the rule in Cutter v. Powell (that contracts must be entirely complete) – for example:

◆ where there is acceptance of partial performance of the contract; and

◆ where one party prevents the other from performance of their duties.

Test yourself 4.2

What would constitute adequate consideration for a contract to be binding?

---

4. Breach of conditions

The conditions of a contract should be fulfilled completely. In the event that a condition of a contract is not fulfilled by either party, the person who did not fulfil their promise is said to be in breach of the contract.

The innocent party to a breached contract could sue the party that did not fulfil its obligations for the standard remedy of damages. The Limitation Act 1980 states that 'An action founded on simple contract shall not be brought after the expiration of six years from the date on which the cause of action accrued'.

If breaches are absolutely fundamental, it may be possible for the aggrieved party to terminate the contract.

An anticipatory breach is an unequivocal indication that a party will not perform its obligations when performance is due. In such an instance, the party that has fulfilled its promise may treat such a breach as immediate and terminate the contract before the breach actually takes place.

5. Remedies for breach of contract

Damages are the standard common law remedy. There are, however, occasions where an award of damages would provide insufficient compensation. In these circumstances, the court can award an equitable remedy.

5.1 Damages

The purpose of damages is to put the innocent party in the position that they would have been in if there had been no breach of the contract.

The aggrieved party to a breached contract is obliged to limit their damages so far as they are able. Only damages that are not too remote may be recovered. The injured party cannot recover damages for every kind of loss they have suffered. The breach might cause a chain reaction of events and clearly the contract breaker cannot be held responsible for all of the consequences of their breach.

5.2 Equitable remedies

specific performance
An equitable remedy that a court may make which orders the parties to the contract to fulfil their obligations under it.

injunction
A judicial order that restrains a person from doing something or orders someone do to something.

Mareva injunction
An order of the court which prevents a defendant to an action from disposing of the assets or transferring them from the jurisdiction.

rescission
The revocation or cancellation of a contract. The effect is to bring the parties to the contract back to the position that they were in before the contract was effected.

Equitable remedies include **specific performance**, **injunction**, a **Mareva injunction** or **rescission**. An equitable remedy cannot be granted if the claimant has acted unfairly. This is the equitable maxim that 'he who comes to equity must come with clean hands'.

Specific performance

The court may make an order for 'specific performance' which orders the parties to fulfil their obligations under the contract. An example of a circumstance where the court may order 'specific performance' may be where unique or limited edition goods are involved. However, specific performance will not be awarded where damages would be an adequate remedy.

Injunction

An injunction is a judicial order that restrains a person from doing something or orders someone to do something.

Mareva injunction

A Mareva injunction is sometimes referred to as an asset freezing order. It is a court order which freezes assets, thereby preventing a defendant to an action from disposing of the assets or transferring them from the jurisdiction.

Rescission

Rescission restores the parties to the position they were in before the contract was entered into. It is for this reason that rescission is not usually an option where there has been substantial performance of the contract.

Test yourself 4.3

Outline two equitable remedies for breach of a contract.

Chapter summary

◆ A contract is an agreement between parties that is made with the intention for it to be legally binding and supported by consideration. It can be made in any form, although some contracts must be made in writing.

◆ The essential elements of a contract are agreement (made by an offer and acceptance), consideration and intention to create legal relations. To ensure that the contract is enforceable, the parties to it must have legal capacity to contract and the contract must not be illegal.

◆ An offer is a definite expression of willingness to be bound on specific terms without further negotiations. The mere supply of information is not considered to be an offer, neither is an invitation to treat.

◆ Acceptance of an offer is an unconditional agreement to all of the terms of the offer. An offer must be accepted before it has been terminated and acceptance must be communicated to the offeror (although there are exceptions to this rule).

◆ Consideration is defined in Currie v. Misa (1875) as being 'some right, interest, profit or benefit accruing to one party or some forbearance, detriment, loss or responsibility given, suffered or undertaken by the other'.

◆ Consideration must be provided by both parties to a contract; it need not be adequate but must be sufficient. Past consideration is not sufficient consideration and performance of existing duties is also not sufficient consideration.

◆ The parties to a contract must have had an intention that the arrangement would be legally binding.

◆ Contracts that are deemed to be illegal cannot be enforced.

◆ The general rule is that contracts must be performed in their entirety, unless there is acceptance of partial performance of the contract or where one party prevents the other from performance of their duties.

◆ In the event that conditions of a contract are not fulfilled by either party, the innocent party can sue the other party for the standard remedy of damages (providing they bring an action before the expiration of six years from the date on which the cause of action happened).

◆ Where damages would not provide sufficient compensation, the court can award equitable remedies such as specific performance, injunction, Mareva injunction or rescission.

Part Three

Taxation

After studying this part, students will have gained an appreciation of the complexity of taxation and the need for expert tax advice. Students will be able to distinguish between direct and indirect taxes, and will be able to discuss the principles of the main types of taxes that affect individuals and entities such as companies, trusts, partnerships and foundations and the European Savings Tax Directive. Students will gain an understanding of tax planning concepts and gain an understanding of the general principles of residence and domicile, and how these may impact on the basis that individuals may be taxed under (for example, the arising basis or the remittance basis). Students will be able to discuss the use of offshore entities to reduce taxation. Students will gain an awareness of the important difference between tax avoidance and tax evasion, and will gain an understanding of the OECD's work on harmful tax practices and on the internationally agreed standard of exchange of information on tax matters.

Learning outcomes

At the end of this part, students will be able to:

◆ discuss the need for expert tax advice;

◆ distinguish between direct and indirect taxes;

◆ discuss the principles of income tax, corporation tax, capital gains tax, inheritance tax and other taxes;

◆ explain the aim of the European Savings Tax Directive;

◆ discuss tax planning concepts;

◆ discuss the general principles of residence, ordinary residence, domicile and the concept of being deemed domiciled;

◆ discuss the arising basis of taxation and the remittance basis of taxation;

◆ discuss the use of offshore entities to reduce tax;

◆ discuss the principle of residence in relation to companies;

◆ understand the principles of corporation tax;

◆ discuss the taxation of trusts, partnerships and foundations;

◆ explain the difference between tax avoidance and tax evasion;

◆ discuss OECD's harmful tax practices initiative and the internationally agreed standard on exchange of information on tax matters; and

◆ discuss transfer pricing issues.

Chapter five
Different taxes and their implications

List of topics

Introduction

This chapter outlines the need for expert advice in the complex area of taxation. Some of the many types of taxation that an offshore administrator may encounter are outlined briefly. The main taxes that are most common to individuals and entities (income tax, corporation tax, capital gains tax and inheritance tax) are discussed in more detail, mainly in relation to how each tax affects individuals (taxation of entities is discussed in Chapter 6). The chapter outlines the European Savings Tax Directive, which has been implemented in some offshore centres despite there being no obligation for the centres to do so. The chapter concludes with a discussion of basic tax planning concepts, including residence and domicile, and outlines how non-UK-domiciled individuals (or those who are not ordinarily resident in the UK) may choose to be taxed on the special remittance basis rather than the more usual arising basis of taxation.

1. The need for expert advice

There are many complex rules surrounding taxation that vary depending on the circumstances of an individual (or entity), including their residence, ordinary residence and their domicile. The concept of residence and domicile are not clearly defined rules in statute and as a result there is no certainty about the way that all individuals will be treated for tax purposes. Court cases have decided the rules to some extent; however, the circumstances of the cases do not apply to everyone's situation. Offshore professionals need to be aware that taxation is a complex issue and each client's circumstances will be different. It is therefore important that offshore service providers appreciate the need for expert advice. It is for this reason that it will generally be the policy of offshore service providers such as trust companies not to provide taxation advice.

There are many myths about the use of offshore centres. Any client who wishes to use an offshore centre for the purposes of reducing liability to taxation should be advised to seek their own tax advice.

The tax rules change every year. Offshore service providers should therefore be conscious that while the structure was appropriate at the time that it was created, it is not necessarily still tax-efficient years later. In order to act in the best interests of beneficiaries and beneficial owners of offshore vehicles, it is important that taxation consequences of services provided are considered and reviewed on an ongoing basis.

It is not the role of offshore trust and company professionals to give tax advice and they are entitled to trust that their clients are honest individuals who have declared all relevant income and gains to their tax authorities. That said, service providers and their employees cannot shut their eyes to the obvious where they suspect tax evasion and must bear in mind their own obligations under their jurisdiction's AML legislation. Dealing with the proceeds of tax evasion or suspected tax evasion in many jurisdictions is dealing with the proceeds of crime.

2. Types of taxes

Taxes are charges levied by the government in order to raise revenue to pay for public services in order to meet the needs of its communities, to ensure that the people are healthy and secure, and to assist those that are in need. Taxes are compulsory.

Although the tax rules differ significantly from jurisdiction to jurisdiction, the types of considerations that offshore service providers pay attention to in the UK will be similar to those required in other major onshore centres. In order to gain an understanding of taxation principles, UK rules are referred to in this chapter.

Natural persons, legal persons and legal arrangements are all subject to tax. The basis of taxation varies depending on the type of person (natural or legal) and the jurisdiction that they are deemed to be resident in, or domiciled in.

The types of taxes that an individual or a company may have to pay include:

◆ income tax (IT);
◆ capital gains tax (CGT);
◆ inheritance tax (IHT);
◆ wealth taxes;
◆ stamp duty; and
◆ value added tax (VAT)

Taxes can be direct taxes, indirect taxes or other taxes such as annual wealth taxes.

Taxes on income can be described as direct taxes. Examples of direct taxes include:

◆ income taxes;
◆ corporation tax;
◆ stamp duty land tax;
◆ stamp duty reserve tax;
◆ inheritance tax; and
◆ capital gains tax.

Indirect taxes are those on expenditure, for example:

◆ VAT;
◆ customs duties;
◆ excise duties; and
◆ insurance premium tax.

While the above-mentioned taxes are common in onshore jurisdictions, as explained in Chapter 1, it is not common to find taxes such as CGT, IHT or VAT in offshore centres. Whether or not such taxes exist in offshore centres, offshore administrators with onshore clients will still need to be familiar with them as their clients and entities under administration (depending on their activity) may be impacted by them.

Where taxes do exist in offshore centres, they are usually only charged on the residents of the jurisdiction and exist at a much lower rate than is charged in onshore jurisdictions.

Test yourself 5.1

Explain the difference between direct and indirect taxes.

2.1 Types of tax systems

Income tax systems include three types: progressive, proportional and regressive.

Progressive

Progressive tax systems are those with a rate of tax that increases as the individual's earnings increase. There is usually a level of income that is exempt from tax followed by tax rates that increase when certain income thresholds are met. The UK has a progressive tax system.

Proportional

Tax systems where there is a flat tax regime can be referred to as proportional tax systems. With the proportional tax system, there is usually an exemption for a certain amount of earned income and then a single rate is charged on the remainder. Offshore centres such as Jersey often have such a taxation system.

Regressive

Regressive tax systems are those where the rate of tax falls as the level of income that is subject to tax rises.

3. Income tax

Income tax (IT) is a tax that is levied on the income that individuals receive over a personal allowance which is income tax exempt. Other entities such as trusts and non-resident companies may also be subject to income tax.

Individuals and other entities such as trusts are usually required to complete an income tax return on an annual basis which declares the amount of income that has been received during the previous fiscal (tax) year.

The fiscal year in the UK starts on 6 April and ends on 5 April each year. Fiscal years differs from jurisdiction to jurisdiction. For example, the Jersey fiscal year runs in line with the calendar year (from 1 January to 31 December).

Administrators in offshore centres should be conscious of the fiscal year in their own jurisdiction as well as that of their client's residence.

In the UK, income tax is a progressive tax, meaning that the amount of income tax payable increases with the level of income of the taxpayer. The rate of income tax that the individual is subject to is determined by the tax band that their earnings fall into. There is a basic rate, a higher rate and an additional rate.

The amount of income tax charged depends on whether the income is earned or unearned income as the two types of income are taxed at different rates and on the level of income received.

3.1 Earned income

earned income
Income that is earned – for example, salary or bonuses from employment or income from a trade or profession or from a pension.

Earned income is income that is earned – for example, salary or bonuses from employment or income from a trade or profession or from a pension.

3.2 Unearned income

Unearned income includes income that is received from sources other than from employment (or a trade or profession), such as:

◆ dividends;

◆ bank interest (or building society interest);

◆ interest on stocks;

◆ royalty payments; and

◆ rental income from investment properties.

Tax on bank interest and dividends are usually 'taxed at source' which means that the tax has already been deducted from the amount received. Where income is taxed at source, basic rate taxpayers will have no further tax to pay; however, higher-rate taxpayers will have more to pay.

Dividends are taxed at three different rates, depending on the level of overall taxable income. Savings income is taxed at four different rates, depending on the individual's overall taxable income.

unearned income
Unearned income includes income that is received from sources other than from employment (or a trade or profession).

4. Corporation tax

Income earned by companies is subject to corporation tax (also known as profits tax in some jurisdictions). Corporation tax is charged on the net income after relevant allowances and reliefs. This tax is discussed further in Chapter 6.

5. Capital gains tax

Capital gains tax (CGT) is a tax on profits or gain that is made when a **chargeable asset** is disposed of (i.e. sold, given away, transferred or exchanged for something else) if it has increased in value and a 'gain' has been made.

Chargeable assets are those that may be subject to CGT when they are disposed of. Current examples of items that attract CGT are:

◆ land;

◆ buildings (not including an individual's main residence);

◆ personal possessions (e.g. artwork or jewellery) worth more than £6,000; and

◆ shares or securities.

There are some assets that are not subject to CGT – these include:

◆ **wasting assets** such as a car;

◆ an individual's main residence;

◆ special investments such as Individual Savings Accounts (ISAs);

◆ UK government bonds (Gilts);

chargeable asset
An asset that may be subject to capital gains tax when it is disposed of (i.e. sold or given away).

wasting asset
An asset that has a limited life and therefore decreases in value over time, e.g. a car or a factory machine.

◆ personal belongings worth £6,000 or less when they are sold; and

◆ money which forms a part of an individual's income for income tax purposes.

There are other disposals that are not subject to CGT – for example, gifts between spouses. Gains made upon the transfer of an asset due to the owner's death are not subject to CGT, although they may be subject to IHT.

Losses made – for example, on the sale of an investment property – can be offset against chargeable gains made on other assets.

chargeable gain
A gain made on the same of an asset that is liable to capital gains tax.

Those who make a **chargeable gain** (i.e. one that is liable to CGT) must complete a self-assessment tax return.

5.1 Who pays capital gains tax?

CGT is payable in the UK by:

◆ individuals who are UK-resident or UK ordinarily resident;

◆ UK-resident trusts; and

◆ non-resident persons trading in the UK through a branch.

Individuals who are UK-resident or ordinarily resident are liable for CGT on their worldwide capital gains.

Individuals who are UK-resident or ordinarily resident but are not UK-domiciled are liable for CGT on gains arising from the disposal of UK assets and are liable to CGT on 'foreign gains' if the proceeds are remitted to the UK.

When deciding whether an asset is a UK or foreign asset, the following is the case.

Table 5.1: Assets and their locations.

Type of asset	Location of asset
Land and buildings	Where the property is physically located
Chattels	Where they are physically located (they can therefore move between countries)
Debts	Where creditor is located
Patents and trademarks	Where they are registered

6. Inheritance tax

Inheritance tax (IHT), also known as estate or death tax, is usually paid on a person's estate when they die.

IHT is payable by the person or persons who inherit the deceased person's assets in circumstances where the estate is valued over a certain threshold also known as the 'nil rate band'. It is therefore very important for an individual with substantial assets to consider any potential IHT liability.

In the UK, IHT is sometimes payable during a person's lifetime when trusts are settled or gifts are made during a person's lifetime – for example, when setting up a trust, tax is payable at half of the death rate. Other gifts are referred to as potentially exempt transfers which, if made during the lifetime of an individual, can reduce the level of tax liability on the estate at the time of death.

Stop and think 5.1

Which of the types of taxes described in section 2 of this chapter are levied in your jurisdiction?

6.1 Exempt transfers

Some transfers are exempt from IHT. These include those which are made to:

◆ a spouse or civil partner;
◆ some national institutions such as museums, universities or the National Trust;
◆ UK political parties (if the party meets certain criteria); and
◆ qualifying charities.

In the UK, each person is allowed to make gifts worth up to a certain value in each tax year which are exempt from IHT. There are also exemptions up to certain limits for other types of gifts, for example, gifts made in consideration of marriage, small gifts, regular gifts (e.g. for birthdays and Christmas).

6.2 Potentially exempt transfers

Any gifts that are made to individuals will be exempt from IHT as long as the donor lives for seven years after making the gift (this is known as the seven-year rule). These gifts are known as Potentially Exempt Transfers (PETs).

An IHT liability will arise in relation to the assets if the donor's estate is worth more than the 'nil rate band'. Taper relief is applied, meaning that the amount of tax payable reduces on a sliding scale.

A person's estate therefore includes their assets at the time of their death and any assets given away within the seven years prior to their death.

Taper relief
If a person dies between three and seven years of making a gift, taper relief is applied. This reduces the percentage of IHT payable on a sliding scale based on the time between the date that the gift was made and the date of death. After seven years, IHT is not payable.

Test yourself 5.2

When is inheritance tax usually payable?

7. Other taxes

7.1 Wealth taxes

Some jurisdictions impose an annual wealth tax on individuals whose assets are valued above a predetermined level on a specific date. As wealth taxes are determined on 'net worth', they can be referred to as 'net worth' taxes. Often the percentage level of wealth tax is low; however, this is not always the case. France is an example of a country where a significant level of the government's revenue arises from 'net worth' taxes. Wealth taxes are not usually a feature in offshore centres.

7.2 Stamp duty

Stamp duty or stamp duty land tax is payable on land and property transactions above a certain value. Stamp duty is also payable on the purchase of shares if the transaction is paper-based (or stamp duty reserve tax if it is a paperless transaction).

7.3 Value added tax

Value added tax (VAT) is charged at a flat rate and is added to the price that is paid for certain goods or services.

VAT is calculated at each level that value is added to an article or service as it progresses to an end user. VAT is therefore an indirect tax on consumption. Over the years, VAT has replaced sales tax in many countries because it is less open to abuse.

VAT is not a common feature of offshore centres and this creates advantages for onshore retailers.

Making it work 5.1: Low Value Consignment Relief (LVCR)

Usually when goods are imported into the EU from a non-EU territory, they are subject to VAT; however, there is an optional exception allowed on shipments of low-value goods. In this respect, the UK allows VAT relief known as 'Low Value Consignment Relief' (LVCR) in respect of goods that are valued at below the threshold of £18.

LVCR allows goods such as CDs and DVDs manufactured in the UK to be exported to the offshore centres such as those located in the Channel Islands and then mailed back to the UK VAT-free. Many well-known retailers such as HMV, WHSmith, Asda, Amazon, Tesco, Dixons, The Hut and Argos are reported to have made use of advantages that operating 'offshore' can offer, securing an advantage over their onshore competitors. This relief led to a very profitable 'fulfilment industry' within the islands; however, its expansion attracted a lot of bad press.

In 2007, Jersey changed its policy to require that e-commerce companies would require Jersey owners and a physical base employing local people. The fulfilment operations of approximately 16 major UK retailers were declined permission to continue to operate from within the Island following the policy change. Guernsey also took steps to limit the abuse; however, a number of UK retailers still operate from within the jurisdiction.

In the budget report for 2011/2012, the government set out that it would reduce LVCR from £18 to £15 from November 2011. It also stated that it 'will explore options with the European Commission to limit the scope of the relief so that it can no longer be exploited for a purpose that it was not intended for'. The government also stated that it will revisit the level of the LVCR in the 2012 budget if discussions with the European Community (EC) do not produce a workable solution to the problem of exploitation of the relief.

7.4 Withholding taxes

Withholding taxes are taxes that are deducted from interest and dividends paid to residents of foreign countries. The investor's country of residence may give some relief against these deductions when it assesses the individual for taxes due. A double taxation agreement between two countries can also reduce the level of withholding tax suffered by an investor.

In some countries – for example, the USA and the UK – there is (for non-residents) no withholding tax on interest-paying investments because they want to encourage overseas investors to purchase government debt and to deposit funds with banks and other interest paying institutions.

8. The European Savings Tax Directive

The European Savings Tax Directive (the EUSTD, sometimes referred to as the EUSD) applies to residents of the EU who have overseas investments.

The ultimate aim of the EUSTD is to enable savings income in the form of interest payments made in one EU member state to beneficial owners resident in another EU member state to be made subject to effective taxation in their country of residence. In most member states, automatic exchange of information has been adopted, although some states were permitted to adopt a withholding tax for a transitional period.

Non-EU jurisdictions, however, had some choice in respect of how they would implement the EUSTD. In the Crown Dependencies, paying agents (service providers that pay interest savings income to EU residents) will usually ask their clients to choose from the following options.

◆ **Retention tax option** – Under this option, the service provider will retain tax at a predetermined rate and pay this to the relevant country's authorities without giving details of the resident to whom the payment relates.

◆ **Voluntary exchange of information** – Under this option, the service provider will not retain tax from savings and will instead provide its own tax authorities with information about the client to whom the interest relates. This option requires the express authorisation of the individual.

◆ **Exemption** – Where a beneficial owner presents to the paying agent a certificate drawn up by the competent authority of their EU member state of residence for tax purposes, the paying agent will not be required to apply the retention tax or exchange of information.

In order to reflect the fact that Crown Dependencies are not part of the EU and not subject to the directive, the term 'retention tax' is used rather than 'withholding tax' as used in the directive. While the Crown Dependencies allow paying agents to offer the above three choices, some paying agents will only offer their customers the 'exchange of information' option.

Test yourself 5.3

What is the aim of the European Savings Tax Directive?

9. Tax planning concepts

Tax laws differ between jurisdictions; however, many countries usually consider factors such as residence, domicile or citizenship when deciding whether or not an individual will be taxed in their jurisdiction. Even where jurisdictions have similar taxes, the rules that they apply will undoubtedly differ.

Other factors that may cause an individual to be fiscally connected to a country may include their employment or the location of assets held. A client may be fiscally connected to more than one jurisdiction.

Different tax rules apply to an individual depending on their residence and their domicile. The rules on residence and domicile differ from jurisdiction to jurisdiction. Tax planning is therefore a complicated area and one for which the clients of offshore service providers will often need to take advice.

9.1 Residence

An individual's residence has a significant bearing on an individual's UK tax liability and determines the basis of taxation to which an individual is subject.

The terms 'residence' and 'ordinarily resident' are not defined in the tax legislation. Today's understanding of these terms has evolved based on legal cases that have been decided by the courts over a long period of time. The court's decisions have not provided clear principles that are applicable to all taxpayers.

Individuals are treated as UK-resident for tax purposes in the following circumstances.

◆ Where they are physically present in the UK for 183 days or more during any tax year.

◆ Where they come to the UK with the intention of living in the UK permanently.

◆ Where they come to the UK temporarily and spend 91 days or more each year in the UK on average for three complete tax years they will become UK-resident from the start of the fourth year.

◆ Where they come to the UK for a purpose which will mean that they remain in the UK for at least two years (whether or not they spend 183 days or more in a particular year in the UK), for example, due to their employment.

◆ Where they usually live in the UK and go abroad for short periods (e.g. business trips or holidays).

In addition to the number of days spent in the UK, there are many other different factors that may also indicate that an individual is resident in the UK including their family, social and business ties, and ownership of UK assets. Clients of offshore centres with UK connections take care to count the number of days that they spend in the UK in order to ensure that they do not become UK resident. Only days where the individual is present in the UK at midnight are counted.

UK-resident individuals are normally taxed on the arising basis, meaning that UK tax is paid on all income as it arises and gains as these accrue wherever they arise in the world. UK-resident but non-domiciled individuals have the choice of whether to use the arising basis of taxation or the remittance basis of taxation.

Ordinarily resident

Ordinary residence for tax purposes is a separate concept from tax residence; however, it also has a bearing on an individual's tax liability. There is no statutory definition of ordinary residence. A person may be resident in the UK for a tax year, for example, because they spent 183 days or more in the UK; however, they are not typically (i.e. ordinarily) resident there. A person is ordinarily resident in the UK if their presence in the UK has a settled purpose and forms a part of their regular and habitual mode of their life.

If a person visits the UK for more than 91 days on average over a period of three complete tax years then they are usually treated as ordinarily resident from the start of the next tax year. It could, however, be clear from the facts that a person is ordinarily resident in the UK from the day that they arrive – for example, if they have entered the UK to live or work for three years or more.

A person who is resident but not ordinarily resident may claim the remittance basis for foreign income and gains if they are not UK-domiciled. In addition, certain tax liabilities (for example, CGT) can apply if a person is not resident in the UK but is ordinarily resident in the UK. Individuals who are not ordinarily resident in the UK but are domiciled in the UK can use the remittance basis in respect of foreign income but cannot use it in respect of foreign gains.

Losing residence
In order to prove that an individual is no longer resident in the UK, they would need to demonstrate that they have severed most ongoing links with the UK and many factors would be relevant to Her Majesty's Revenue & Customs (HMRC) when making their decision as to whether that individual is no longer resident in the UK.

Dual residence
It is possible to be resident in the UK and at the same time be resident for tax purposes in another country. Individuals with 'dual residence' would be taxed in accordance with any double taxation agreement that exists between the individual and the other country.

Double taxation agreements
Different countries have different tax rules. It is therefore possible that a person could become liable to tax in two countries (for example, because of their country/countries of residence and the country where the income and gains arise) on the same income.

In order to avoid the double taxation that would arise in these circumstances, countries such as the UK have negotiated double taxation agreements with a large number of countries. Individuals who find themselves subject to double taxation need to make a claim under the relevant agreement.

HMRC consultation: a statutory definition of tax residence
The government has acknowledged the complexity of the residence rules that have developed over time and as a result, HMRC issued a consultation document in June 2011 entitled 'A statutory definition of tax residence'. The document explains that the rules are vague, complicated and perceived to be subjective. The current position is uncertain and is a deterrent to individuals and businesses looking to invest in the UK. The government is therefore committed to introducing a system of determining residence that is transparent, objective and simple to use, and has proposed a framework for a statutory residence test for individuals only (i.e. companies are not included within the scope). The statutory residence test will supersede all existing legislation, case law and guidance once it has been implemented.

The test has three parts. Part A contains conclusive non-residence factors that would be sufficient to make individuals not resident. Part B contains conclusive factors that would be sufficient in themselves to make an individual resident and Part C contains other connecting factors and day-counting rules which will only apply to individuals whose residence status is not determined by Part A or B. The connecting factors in Part C include factors such as family in the UK, accommodation in the UK and substantive work in the UK. The consultation document also proposes a statutory test for ordinary residence.

9.2 Domicile

Domicile is not defined in tax law. Domicile is distinct from a person's nationality and place of residence. A person's domicile is typically where they have their permanent home.

Everyone must have a domicile. There are three types of domicile:

◆   domicile of origin;

◆   domicile of choice; and

◆   domicile of dependence.

A person's domicile affects their position for income tax and CGT purposes only if they have foreign income and gains. A person's domicile is also relevant for IHT purposes.

Deemed domiciled
The concept of being **deemed domiciled** is relevant for IHT purposes only.

Becoming deemed domiciled for IHT purposes does not impact on a person's income tax or CGT position.

An individual will be deemed domiciled in the UK for a tax year if they have been resident in the UK for any part of the last 17 out of 20 years, including the tax year in question.

deemed domiciled
A person becomes deemed domiciled for IHT purposes if they have been present in the UK for any part of the last 17 out of 20 years including the tax year in question.

Domicile of origin
A person acquires a domicile of origin from their father (unless their parents were not married, in which case the domicile of origin is acquired from the mother) when they are born. This domicile is retained until a person acquires a domicile of choice.

Domicile of choice
To acquire a domicile of choice, a person must leave their current country of domicile and settle in another country. It is not sufficient simply to be present in the jurisdiction of the domicile of choice to acquire it. In order to demonstrate that a person has acquired a new domicile of choice, they would need to provide strong evidence that they intend to leave the UK permanently.

The following factors may be relevant:

◆   an individual's intentions;

◆   an individual's permanent residence;

◆   an individual's business interests;

◆   an individual's social and family interests; and

◆   the property that individual owns.

Domicile of dependence

Until a person has the legal capacity to change their domicile, their domicile follows that of the person on whom they are legally dependent. Before 1974, the married woman automatically acquired her husband's domicile. This is no longer the case.

Test yourself 5.4

What is the difference between an individual's domicile and their residence?

In the budget for 2011, the UK government set out that it recognises that non-domiciled individuals make a valuable contribution to the UK economy and that the current tax rules can discourage them from investing their foreign income and gains in the UK. The government acknowledged that the current rules that determine tax residence for individuals are unclear and complex, and stated that it would consult on the introduction of a statutory definition of residence to provide greater certainty for taxpayers. Some certainty was offered within the budget which stated that after the implementation of the reforms to non-domiciled taxation in April 2012, there will be no other substantive changes to these rules for the remainder of the current Parliament.

10. Basis of taxation

10.1 The arising basis of taxation

arising basis of taxation
Under the arising basis of taxation, a person will pay UK tax on all of their income as it arises and on the gains as they accrue, wherever that income and those gains are in the world.

A person who is resident in the UK is normally taxed on the **arising basis of taxation**. This means that they will pay UK tax on all of their income as it arises and on the gains as they accrue, wherever that income and those gains are in the world.

10.2 The remittance basis of taxation

remittance basis of taxation
Individuals who are non domiciled in the UK (or those who are not ordinarily resident in the UK) pay UK tax only on the amount of their foreign income and gains that they remit to the UK.

The **remittance basis of taxation** is an alternative tax treatment to the arising basis and is available to people who are resident in the UK and who are either non-UK-domiciled or not ordinarily resident in the UK. Individuals who have the option to use the remittance basis of taxation may still choose to use the arising basis of taxation if they so wish.

Under the remittance basis, non-domiciled individuals (or those who are not ordinarily resident in the UK) pay UK tax only on the amount of their foreign income and gains that they bring (or 'remit') to the UK. Tax is still paid on income and gains that accrue in the UK. Individuals who are not ordinarily resident in the UK but are domiciled in the UK can use the remittance basis in respect of foreign income but cannot use it in respect of foreign gains.

If a long-term UK resident (one who has been in the UK for seven out of nine of the previous tax years) decides to claim the remittance basis, they may have to pay the remittance basis charge (RBC). The RBC is an annual tax charge for non-domiciled individuals who have been UK resident for at least seven years and is higher for those who have been UK-resident for 12 years or more.

Chapter summary

◆ Taxes are a charge levied by the government in order to pay for public services and are compulsory.

◆ There are complex rules surrounding taxation that vary depending on an individual's (or an entity's) circumstances including their residence, ordinary residence and their domicile. As the complex rules change (and new rules are introduced) each year, it is important that offshore administrators appreciate the need for expert advice.

◆ The types of taxes that an individual or entity may have to pay include income tax, capital gains tax, inheritance tax, wealth taxes, stamp duty and VAT. Many of the types of taxes found onshore will not be present in offshore centres, although clients of offshore centres may be subject to them and it is therefore important that offshore administrators have an understanding of the taxes and basic tax concepts.

◆ Taxes on income can be described as direct taxes, while taxes on expenditure can be described as indirect taxes.

◆ Tax systems can be progressive (where the rate of tax increases as the individual's earnings increase), proportional (where the amount of tax charged is at a single rate) and regressive (where the amount of tax charged falls as the level of taxable income rises). The UK's system is a progressive system. It is more common in offshore centres for the system to be proportional.

◆ Income tax is a tax that is levied on the income that individuals receive over a personal allowance. Income is levied at different rates depending on whether the income is considered to be earned income or unearned income. Corporation tax is charged on the income of companies.

◆ Capital gains tax is a tax on profits or gains that are made when a chargeable asset is disposed of and a gain as been made. Capital gains tax is charged on UK residents only (and those non-resident persons who trade in the UK through a branch).

◆ Inheritance tax is charged on a person's estate when they die, if the estate is valued over a certain threshold known as a 'nil rate band'. Inheritance tax can also be payable during a person's lifetime – for example, when an individual settles a trust. Some transfers are exempt from inheritance tax and others are potentially exempt, meaning that the gift will be free of inheritance tax providing the donor lives for seven years after making the gift and that the gift was not a gift with reservation.

◆ Some offshore centres have implemented the European Savings Tax Directive, even though they were not under an obligation to do so, which applies to residents of the EU with overseas investments. The ultimate aim of the directive is to enable savings income in the form of interest in one EU member state to beneficial owners resident in another to be made subject to effective taxation in their country of residence.

◆ In many jurisdictions, concepts such as a person's residence and domicile are key factors in deciding whether or not they will be subject to taxation in their jurisdiction. In the UK, the term 'residence' is very important although it is not defined in the tax legislation and instead, today's understanding of these terms has evolved based on rulings of the court. The term 'domicile' is similarly not defined in legislation and is considered typically to be where an individual has their permanent home.

◆ Individuals in the UK are usually subject to tax on the arising basis, which means that they will pay UK tax on all of their income as it arises and on the gains as they accrue, wherever that income and those gains are in the world. Individuals who are not domiciled in the UK or who are not ordinarily resident there may choose instead to use the special remittance basis of taxation, which means that tax is only paid on income when it is remitted into the UK.

Chapter six
Residence, domicile, and tax implications

List of topics

1. The use of offshore entities to reduce taxation
2. Taxation of companies
3. Taxation of trusts
4. Taxation of partnerships and foundations
5. Tax avoidance and tax evasion
6. The OECD
7. Transfer pricing

Introduction

This chapter begins with a discussion of the use of offshore entities to reduce taxation before outlining how a company's residence is determined and discussing the important issues surrounding management and control. Corporation tax, to which companies are subject, is explained. The chapter then discusses the taxation of trusts, which includes the inheritance tax charges that can arise on the creation of the trust and on each 10-year anniversary, and the exit charges that arise when funds are paid out of the trust. The taxation of partnerships is briefly explained as is the uncertain position of the taxation of foundations. The chapter outlines the important difference between tax avoidance and tax evasion, and some circumstances in which offshore administrators may find themselves inadvertently assisting clients to evade taxation. The OECD's contribution to the global fight against tax evasion is discussed, including its model agreement on exchange of information and its guidelines to address the transfer pricing problem.

1. The use of offshore entities to reduce taxation

As discussed in Chapter 5, tax planning, particularly when it involves the use of offshore entities or structures, is a very complex area that requires expert advice from a taxation professional.

In some circumstances, offshore entities (such as trusts and companies) can be used to retain income or profits, thus deferring a tax liability until distributions are made which could be at a time when the client's basic rate to tax has fallen. Tax deferral is a key feature of tax planning.

Chapter 5 also discussed how non-residents of a jurisdiction are often taxed more favourably than its residents. Offshore companies incorporated in a low tax jurisdiction (and managed and controlled there) could hold the assets or undertake a specific activity, thus allowing the client to benefit from the non-resident status of the company, although **anti-avoidance legislation** must always be taken into consideration.

anti-avoidance legislation
Legislation that has been introduced in order to minimise the opportunities to minimise taxation via the use of offshore centres, particularly where the transaction has no purpose other than the minimisation of taxation.

An example of how offshore trusts and companies have been used together to reduce a taxation liability is where funds are settled into a trust and then loaned on a commercial (i.e. on an 'arm's length') basis to an underlying company for the specific purpose of enabling the company to purchase a property that will be rented out. When the rent is received, the cost of repaying the loan to the trust can be offset as an expense against the rental receipts, thus reducing the taxable income of the company.

Over the years, anti-avoidance legislation has been introduced in onshore jurisdictions which is designed to reduce the opportunities available to its residents (or domiciled individuals) to avoid taxation via the use of offshore entities by preventing certain types of financial activity from receiving favourable tax treatment.

Every time one tax 'loophole' becomes unavailable, tax specialists work hard to identify new opportunities. The government has a difficult task in keeping up with the strategies that are devised and it has to balance legislation with rules that encourage wealthy people to live and remain in the UK, and incentivise businesses to operate from within the UK.

2. Taxation of companies

2.1 Residence of companies

Companies that are incorporated in the UK are usually considered to be resident in the UK. For foreign incorporated companies (e.g. those incorporated in offshore centres), a company is considered to be resident wherever the central management and control actually abides (as established by De Beers Consolidated Mines Ltd v. Howe).

The significance of a company's residence is as follows.

◆ Companies that are resident in the UK are subject to corporation tax (discussed in section 2.3 of this chapter) on the whole of its chargeable profits on a worldwide basis.

◆ Companies which are not resident in the UK are liable to corporation tax only if they carry on a trade in the UK through a permanent establishment.

◆ Non-resident companies may also be liable to UK income tax (rather than corporation tax) on non-trading income.

2.2 Management and control

Offshore service providers are often directors of companies that are incorporated outside of the UK and managed and controlled outside of the UK (i.e. from within the offshore centre). Such companies are considered to be non-resident.

Where it is the case that management and control must be outside of the UK for a structure to be tax-efficient, it is very important that service providers explain this concept to the client (who may be the beneficial owner or beneficiary of a trust that owns the company) and ensure that the client understands that they will not be able to take part in the management or decision making of the company.

It can be difficult for offshore service providers to keep their client from interfering in the affairs of the company. Offshore directors who simply follow their client's wishes run the risk of allowing their client to become a **shadow director** (i.e. one who has not been formally appointed but who is deemed in law to be a director due to the function that they are fulfilling). If such a client is resident in the UK, it could be argued that the company is managed and controlled from within the UK and that the company should therefore be paying corporation tax on the whole of its profits on a worldwide basis. Management and control must therefore be firmly with the offshore directors.

shadow director
One who has not been formally appointed but who is deemed in law to be a director due to the function that they are fulfilling.

All too often, offshore administrators face the situation where an onshore client decides to become involved in the affairs of the company, sometimes signing documentation on behalf of the company or negotiating major deals on its behalf and failing to keep the offshore directors informed.

In some circumstances, offshore directors have good reason to involve or take advice from the client; for example, they may be an expert on the business that the company is engaged in and the client's opinions, contacts and general involvement is of great assistance to the directors. It is perfectly acceptable for directors to involve their clients in such circumstances; however, it is vital that the terms of such an arrangement are documented (for example, perhaps the client could be engaged as a consultant and with an agreement that makes it clear what the scope of their involvement is and providing for the client to be properly remunerated for their services. It is also important to ensure it is well documented that decisions are in fact made by the directors and not the client.

Offshore directors will have taken some comfort from the decision in the case known as Wood v. Holden (2006).

Case law 6.1: Wood v. Holden (2006)

In this case, the Inland Revenue had decided that Eulalia Holding BV (Eulalia), a company incorporated in the Netherlands, was resident in the UK and if that was correct, capital gains tax in a large sum was payable by Mr and Mrs Wood. The sole director of the Eulalia Holding BV was AA Trust (a part of ABN AMRO in the Netherlands), which took decisions in relation to a transaction in Amsterdam. The Inland Revenue argued that ABN AMRO did not in fact take the decisions but did what it was told to do by Mr Wood. The court of appeal decided that 'the transaction was conducted by AA Trust as the director of Eulalia and in the Netherlands. AA Trust might have had every incentive to carry it out; but it had the right to refuse if it wished, and had the power to do so. In my judgement Eulalia was and remained in the Netherlands, and was not resident in the United Kingdom'. In essence, the case demonstrates that although offshore directors may make decisions that are ill informed, what is important in determining management and control is that the decision lies with the directors.

Test yourself 6.1

Where is a company usually considered to be resident?

2.3 Corporation tax

Corporation tax is a tax on the taxable profits of limited companies and some unincorporated organisations.

Taxable profits for corporation tax include:

◆ profit from taxable income such as trading profits and investment profits; and

◆ capital gains (known as chargeable gains, for corporation tax purposes).

Offshore service providers often appoint tax advisers to deal with the tax authorities and to complete corporation tax returns on their behalf.

Companies that are resident in the UK are subject to corporation tax on the whole of their worldwide income and gains. Companies that are non-resident in the UK pay corporation tax only if it carries on a trade in the UK through a permanent establishment.

The amount of tax payable is usually a percentage of the taxable profits of the company. The profits that are chargeable to corporation tax will not usually match the amount of profit that is shown in the accounts of the company, as certain expenses charged to the profit and loss account (e.g. entertainment expenses) are not allowed as a deduction for corporation tax purposes.

3. Taxation of trusts

A trust will normally be considered to be resident wherever the majority of its trustees are resident. If all trustees are resident outside of the UK, the trust will not be considered to be resident in the UK. If, however, there is a mixture of resident and non-resident trustees, the trust will be resident unless the settlor was non-resident (and non-ordinarily resident) and non-domiciled. Trusts that are resident in the UK are liable to income tax on their worldwide income.

Non-resident trusts are treated differently depending on the type of trust (e.g. whether they are discretionary trusts or life interest settlements) and depending on the residence status of the settlors or beneficiaries.

In the same way that offshore directors of companies that claim to be non-resident in the UK must ensure that the management and control of the company is firmly with them, offshore trustees must ensure that the assets of the trust are properly vested in them and that they (rather than the client) are in control of them. This is important in order to ensure that the trust cannot be considered to be a sham (i.e. that the settlor never really gave their assets away and continues to control them) and to ensure that gifts with reservation (discussed in section 2.1 of this chapter) are not created (unless this is intended) or there may be unintended taxation consequences. Trustees will need to consider their dealings with settlor beneficiaries in order to avoid any problems arising. For example, it may be better to charge the client a market rent for the use of a property (thereby introducing funds into the trust) rather than create a gift with reservation. In such circumstances, offshore administrators must also ensure that any relevant documentation is also in place (e.g. an adequate tenancy agreement).

When a beneficiary receives distributions from the trust assets, this does not usually result in a liability on the trustees; however, it may result in a tax liability for the beneficiary. Trustees should consider the impact of taxation when deciding whether to make distributions (and whether they should distribute capital or income). The beneficiary should be informed that they may be subject to tax on the distribution and be advised to take their own tax advice. The type of trust, the residence and domicile of the settlor and the beneficiaries may also result in the settlor being liable to tax.

In general, capital distributions to beneficiaries will be free of liability to income tax while income distributions are likely to result in a liability. That said, the tax authorities can view regular capital distributions as income. It is therefore very important to keep income and capital entirely separate in order that it can always be shown whether or not a distribution is in fact capital or income as may be the case. This is the reason that separate bank accounts for capital and income are maintained for offshore clients and that capital and income should not be mixed.

As is always the case with taxation, it is important to take (or advise the client to take) taxation advice.

As a trust is not a legal person, any tax liability is assessed on the trustees (rather than the trust itself) and due to be paid by the trustee.

3.1 Inheritance tax charges in relation to trusts

Gifts to discretionary trusts are chargeable lifetime transfers and immediately subject to an IHT charge of 20% over the nil rate band. If the donor does not survive for seven years after settling the trust, IHT at the usual death rate will be payable.

Offshore trusts can therefore be a useful way to reduce the level of IHT that is payable from a person's estate, providing the assets are gifted in a timely manner.

For example, if the assets were not held in a trust and were instead held by an individual, UK IHT would be due on the individual's death in respect of any UK assets and if the individual was deemed domiciled in the UK, IHT would be due in respect of their worldwide assets. Wealthy individuals can therefore reduce their IHT liability by giving away their assets.

If an asset is given away, for example, to an offshore trust, but an interest is kept in the asset (e.g. a settlor settles their house into the trust but continues to live in it rent free), then this gift is known as a **gift with reservation** and is not a potentially exempt transfer. Such a gift would still form a part of the person's estate upon their death.

Excluded property trusts

Non-UK-domiciled individuals (who have not yet been deemed domiciled in the UK) have been able to create **excluded property trusts** which are trusts that are created with non-UK situs assets (i.e. assets that are not situated in the UK).

Such trusts receive favourable IHT treatment. To the extent that non UK assets are held within such a trust, these assets will be exempt from IHT and to the extent that non-UK assets are held, the 10-year anniversary charge to IHT and the exit charges that are charged when property leaves the trust can be avoided.

If assets were not held in trust, the IHT would become payable upon the death of the individual on their UK assets and if they had become deemed domiciled in the UK, tax would be due in respect of their worldwide assets.

Ten-year anniversary charge

The assets of discretionary trusts (and some other trusts) may give rise to IHT charges every 10 years and a charge when the property leaves the trust (known as an exit charge). To the extent that an excluded property holds non-UK situs assets, these charges will not arise. With careful tax planning, charges on UK situs assets may also be avoided.

Offshore administrators should ensure that they have diarised to consider what steps may need to be taken prior to the 10-year anniversary of trusts under their administration in order to reduce the IHT charge that becomes payable. They will also need to remember to take active steps to declare and pay the tax due to HMRC, which may be unaware of the existence of the trust.

gift with reservation
A gift whereby the donor retains an interest in the asset (this could involve retaining a benefit or control of the asset).

excluded property trust
Excluded property trusts are those created by non-UK-domiciled individuals (who have not yet been deemed domiciled in the UK) with non-UK situs assets. Such trusts receive favourable IHT treatment.

Test yourself 6.2

What is meant by the term 'gift with reservation'?

4. Taxation of partnerships and foundation

4.1 Partnerships

Partners of a general partnership are required to pay income tax on their share of the partnership's profits. A nominated partner completes a partnership tax return showing each partner's share of the profit or losses.

With limited partnerships, limited partners are taxed on their share of the profits as if they had carried out the activity of the Limited Partnership alone.

Although a Limited Liability Partnership (LLP) is regarded as a corporate body, for tax purposes, it is treated in the same way as a general partnership. LLPs are transparent for tax purposes, which means that they are not taxed in their own right. Instead each member is assessed to tax as if they were members of a general partnership (i.e. they are treated as having carried on the activities of the LLP in proportion to their membership).

For capital gains tax purposes, the partners are charged on the disposal of their interests in chargeable assets of the partnership where gains arise.

4.2 Foundations

Foundations are incorporated bodies, although they differ somewhat from companies. UK tax law does not specifically deal with entities such as foundations. It is not yet clear whether HMRC will tax foundations as corporate bodies or as settlements for each of the main taxes.

Tax advisers have stated that it is likely that the residence of foundations will be determined as if they were companies (i.e. resident wherever they are managed and controlled).

Those administering offshore foundations should be aware that anti-avoidance legislation applied to offshore trusts and foreign companies may well be applied to foundations.

At this time, UK residents, whether domiciled or not, should only consider using a foundation with caution and with the assistance of an appropriately qualified tax adviser.

5. Tax avoidance and tax evasion

5.1 Tax avoidance

Tax avoidance involves the legitimate minimisation (or avoidance) of a taxation liability. In a House of Lords decision (Inland Revenue Commissioners v. Duke of Westminster 1936), Lord Tomlin commented that:

> Every man is entitled if he can to arrange his affairs so that the tax attaching under the appropriate Acts is less than it otherwise would be. If he succeeds in ordering them so as to secure that result, then, however unappreciative the Commissioners of Inland Revenue or his fellow taxpayers may be of his ingenuity, he cannot be compelled to pay an increased tax.

The UK and other onshore jurisdictions have sought to minimise the opportunities for tax avoidance by the implementation of 'anti-avoidance legislation' that is designed to remove the potential to use any arrangements that are purely used for the avoidance of taxation and involves using the tax laws to gain an advantage that Parliament did not intend.

In March 2011, the government published a document entitled 'Tackling Tax Avoidance'. The document explains that the government inherited a tax system with a tax gap of around £40 billion and that more than a sixth of that is due to tax evasion and a further sixth is estimated to be due to tax avoidance. The report sets out that 'being open for business does not mean being open to tax avoidance' and reiterates that where the government sees tax avoidance, it will crack down on it.

Test yourself 6.3

What is meant by the term 'tax avoidance'?

5.2 Tax evasion

Tax evasion, in contrast to tax avoidance, involves the illegal activity of evading a tax liability that is otherwise due and payable. Tax evasion could simply involve an individual failing to declare to the relevant tax authority their income, gains or profits that would be liable to tax, resulting in a lower tax bill than would have otherwise been incurred. Tax evasion may involve the failure to declare income or gains received in respect of an offshore interest bearing bank account or the making of a fraudulent return by under-declaring income to the authorities in their country of residence.

Offshore administrators could find themselves inadvertently assisting clients to evade taxation in a number of circumstances and for a number of reasons. For example:

◆ Aggressive tax avoidance schemes can become superseded by anti-avoidance legislation as the tax legislation changes or become tax-inefficient when the legislation changes each year. Administrators that do not keep up with changes or check the tax efficiency of the structures under their administration risk facilitating tax evasion.

◆ Tax advice may be perfectly adequate and outline clear advantages to the client in certain circumstances; however, the administrator then fails to administer the case in accordance with the advice which can have adverse consequences.

◆ Credit cards drawn on an offshore trust or company provide clients with access to funds in their home jurisdiction without them needing to receive funds into personal bank accounts in their own jurisdiction. This is obviously open to abuse and offshore administrators should seek to understand any request for a credit card.

As offshore administrators do not necessarily understand the taxation advantages of using an offshore centre, there is a risk that they take a 'tick box' approach when they are in receipt of tax advice, simply filing the advice and taking comfort from the fact that they have received it. For example:

◆ They do not check the adequacy of the tax advice. Administrators should ensure that they read the tax advice to ensure that, on the face of it, it makes sense and is likely to be adequate. Tax advice that specifically states that it does not cover, for example, the client's country of residence or domicile may not give a full picture of the client's taxation circumstances.

◆ The suitability of the tax adviser is a risk factor to consider. A tax adviser who will produce a document that clearly states the adviser is not an expert in the tax laws in the jurisdiction that the document purports to give advice in relation to should be viewed with caution.

◆ Offshore administrators sometimes find themselves with tax advice that outlines advantages to their client on a particular basis (for example, that the client is resident or domiciled in a certain jurisdiction). If it is clear to the administrator from their dealings with the client that this basis is not correct, this should be questioned.

While it is not necessary for offshore administrators to obtain tax advice in relation to every client relationship, it is good practice to consider obtaining tax advice, especially if the client cites tax reasons for the business relationship or informs the administrator that they have already taken tax advice. Using a fiscal excuse to explain away a transaction which should invoke an administrator's suspicion is very convenient as administrative staff do not always have an understanding of taxation.

In Switzerland and Luxembourg, the test of predicate criminality within their anti-money laundering legislation excludes tax evasion. The OECD and the international community is forcing them to amend their approach. The Financial Action Tax Force (FATF) Annual Report for 2009–2010 has outlined that tax crime as a predicate offence for money laundering is a priority issue within the FATF recommendations that are currently under review by the FATF.

Making it work 6.1: Tackling tax evasion

The UK government has made the tackling of tax evasion and the recovering of funds from secrecy jurisdictions a priority in recent years.

The Liechtenstein Disclosure Facility (LDF)

Under an agreement signed in August 2009 between the UK and Liechtenstein governments, people with unpaid tax linked to investments or assets in Liechtenstein can settle their tax liability under a special arrangement which will run from 1 September 2009 until 31 March 2015. Under the arrangement, tax offences are guaranteed not to be prosecuted, there is a penalty of 10% and tax is only assessed from April 1999 onwards. The agreement also requires 'financial intermediaries' in Liechtenstein to be satisfied that their UK customers have been declaring their Liechtenstein investments to HMRC in future.

The Swiss Agreement

On 24 August 2011, HMRC announced that 'a historic agreement' had been reached between the UK and Switzerland to tackle tax evasion by those who have abused Swiss banking secrecy.

Under the terms of the agreement, UK taxpayers who have not paid their taxes will be subject to a significant one-off deduction of between 19% and 34% to settle past tax liabilities. As a gesture of good faith, Switzerland agreed to make an up-front payment to Britain of CHF (Swiss francs) 500m. In addition, a new information-sharing provision allows HMRC to find out when Swiss accounts are held by UK residents and a new withholding tax of 48% on investment income and 27% on gains will be introduced from 2013 which will ensure that UK residents with Swiss bank accounts are taxed in future. The withholding tax will not apply if the taxpayer authorises a full disclosure of their affairs to HMRC.

George Osborne, the Chancellor of the Exchequer, was reported to have said:

> Tax evasion is wrong at the best of times, but in economic circumstances like this it means that hard-pressed law-abiding taxpayers are forced to pay even more. That is why this Coalition Government made it a priority to go after those who don't pay their fair share. We will be as tough on the richest who evade tax as on those who cheat on benefits. The days when it was easy to stash the profits of tax evasion in Switzerland are over.

Many have commented that the deal with Switzerland will encourage tax evaders to move their funds to Liechtenstein instead to take advantage of the LDF.

6. The OECD

The Organisation for Economic Co-operation and Development (OECD) was formed on 30 September 1961 and is an international organisation which states that its mission is to promote policies that will improve the economic and social well-being of people around the world. There are 34 member states. A representative from each member state plus a representative from the European Commission makes up the OECD council, which has the power to make decisions on behalf of the organisation. The UK is a member of the OECD.

The OECD provides a forum in which governments can work together to share experiences and seek solutions to common problems. Tax evasion and what the OECD deems to be harmful tax practices are a problem that the OECD has been addressing for many years.

6.1 'Harmful Tax Competition'

The OECD published a report in 1998 entitled 'Harmful Tax Competition: An Emerging Global Issue'. The report identified jurisdictions that it deemed to be tax havens. In deciding whether a jurisdiction was a tax haven, the lack of effective exchange of information was a key criterion.

In 2000, the OECD published a list of over 40 jurisdictions that met the criteria for tax havens set out in the 1998 report.

In mid-2002, it published a list of uncooperative tax havens which did not make commitments to the exchange of information. Each of the jurisdictions on the list made the relevant commitments to implement the OECD standard and as a result, the last three jurisdictions (Andorra, Liechtenstein and Monaco) were removed from the list in May 2009.

6.2 Exchange of information

The OECD views transparency and effective information exchange as essential in enabling countries to apply and enforce their tax laws. The OECD's focus on transparency and effective exchange of information is designed to ensure that a legal framework is in place to allow jurisdictions to cooperate with each other without violating their own laws.

The standards of transparency and effective exchange of information that have been developed by the OECD are primarily contained in Article 26 of the OECD Model Tax Convention and the 2002 Model Agreement on Exchange of Information on Tax Matters.

6.3 The OECD's Model Tax Convention

The model tax convention creates an obligation to exchange information that is relevant to the correct application of a tax convention as well as for the purposes of the administration and enforcement of domestic tax laws of the contracting states. Article 26 of the OECD Model Tax Convention provides the most widely accepted legal basis for bilateral exchange of information for tax purposes. More than 3,000 bilateral treaties are based on the Model Convention.

The internationally agreed tax standard developed by the OECD in conjunction with non-OECD countries (and endorsed by the UN and G20) requires exchange of information on requests in all tax matters for the administration and enforcement of domestic tax law without regard to a domestic tax interest requirement or bank secrecy for tax purposes.

Austria, Belgium, Luxembourg and Switzerland, which are all secrecy jurisdictions, initially indicated that they had reservations to Article 26. However, after succumbing to international pressures in March 2009, each of these countries notified the OECD that they were withdrawing their reservation.

Where information is exchanged, it is subject to strict confidentiality rules and the information that is exchanged may only be used for the purposes provided for in the convention. Only information that is relevant may be exchanged; the requesting state should also have pursued all domestic means to access the requested information except those that would give rise to disproportionate difficulties.

6.4 The OECD Model Agreement on Exchange of Information on Tax Matters

The OECD Global Forum Working Group on Effective Exchange of Information ('the Working Group') developed a model agreement on exchange of information on tax matters. The Working Group consisted of representatives from OECD member countries as well as delegates from many offshore centres including Aruba, Bermuda, Bahrain, the Cayman Islands, Cyprus, the Isle of Man, Malta, the Mauritius, the Netherlands Antilles, the Seychelles and San Marino. The Agreement represents the standard of effective exchange of information for the purposes of the OECD's initiative on harmful tax practices.

When a jurisdiction has signed 12 agreements on exchange of information with jurisdictions that meet the OECD standard, they are considered to have substantially implemented the agreed tax standard. The OECD has, however, stated that it will take into account other matters such as the jurisdictions with which the agreements have been signed (for example, a tax haven that has signed 12 agreements with other tax havens is unlikely to pass the threshold). The OECD may also take into account a jurisdiction's willingness to continue to sign agreements after it has reached the threshold.

Stop and think 6.1

Consider the position of an offshore service provider whose client has stated that they are considering making a disclosure under a facility similar to the Liechtenstein Disclosure Facility mentioned in 'Making it work 6.1' in relation to his offshore accounts. What factors may the service provider need to consider if the closure date for the disclosure passes, but the service provider has not been requested to provide the client with relevant financial information in order to enable them to make a disclosure?

7. Transfer pricing

Whenever goods are sold or services are provided, a price is charged by the seller (or provider) and a price is paid by the buyer (or receiver of the service). The prices that are agreed upon determine the taxable profits (or losses) of any business.

Where parties to a transaction are connected (e.g. they are both part of the same group of companies or the transaction is between an individual and a company which they own), any price set in relation to the sale or transfer of assets or goods between them will not be determined by market forces as would be the case if they were not connected (i.e. if the transaction was an 'arm's length' transaction).

The price that is agreed between two connected parties is known as the **transfer price**. When set between connected parties, this does not impact on the wealth of the common owner; however, it may, where the two connected parties are located in different jurisdictions, incentivise the owner to structure the business so that profits are earned in the jurisdiction that pays the lowest rate of tax. This causes an unfair division of taxable profit between the jurisdictions.

transfer price
The price that is agreed between two connected parties for the sale of goods or services.

The transfer of goods and services within multinational enterprises is a significant part of world trade and the transfer pricing issue, which can artificially shift a tax liability from one jurisdiction to another, is therefore of interest to the OECD.

In order to solve the transfer pricing problem, the OECD has issued transfer pricing guidelines on the issue and has endorsed the 'arm's length principle' (which is internationally recognised) which requires the actual terms of a contract to be replaced by the terms that would have been achieved if the transaction was undertaken at arm's length (i.e. between unconnected parties) and the profits recalculated accordingly when determining the tax liability. The guidelines also address the issue of minimising double taxation that can occur when multinationals operate. The UK has implemented the OECD's 'arm's length' principle.

The application of this principle involves hypothetically replacing the actual terms of the transaction (e.g. the price) with terms that are considered to be arm's length and recalculating the profits that will be subject to tax on this basis.

Test yourself 6.4

What is the 'transfer pricing' problem?

Chapter summary

◆ Offshore entities can be used to provide opportunities to minimise the amount of taxation payable by offshore clients; however, this is a complex area that requires expert advice from a tax professional.

◆ The residence of a company is considered to be wherever it is managed and controlled.

◆ The residence of a company is significant as companies that are resident in the UK are subject to corporation tax on the whole of their chargeable profits on a worldwide basis, whereas non-resident companies are liable to corporation tax only if they carry on a trade in the UK through a permanent establishment. Corporation tax is a tax on the taxable profits of a limited company.

◆ Where it is essential for the management and control of an offshore company to be outside of the UK in order to achieve tax efficiency, it is vital that management and control is firmly with the offshore directors. Offshore administrators will need to ensure that their clients understand this from the outset of the relationship.

◆ Trusts are considered to be resident wherever the majority of its trustees are resident.

◆ Inheritance tax charges can arise on the creation of certain types of trust, during its existence (for example, on each 10-year anniversary) and exit charges may arise when funds leave the trust.

◆ Partners of partnerships, even those that are considered to be corporate bodies, are required to pay income tax on their share of the partnership's profits.

◆ UK tax legislation does not specifically deal with entities such as foundations and it is not entirely clear yet whether HMRC will tax them as corporate bodies or as settlements.

◆ Tax avoidance involves the legitimate minimisation (or avoidance) of a tax liability. In recent years, the UK has introduced anti-avoidance legislation in order to minimise the opportunities for tax avoidance, especially where arrangements are used purely for the avoidance of taxation.

◆ Tax evasion is the illegal activity of evading a tax liability that is otherwise due and payable. Tax evasion could simply involve the failure by an individual to declare to the relevant tax authority their income, gains or profit that would otherwise be liable to tax.

◆ The OECD has been addressing the problem of tax evasion for many years, beginning with its 1998 report entitled 'Harmful Tax Competition: An Emerging Global Issue'. The international community has put pressure on jurisdictions (particularly those seen as secrecy jurisdictions) and has sought commitments to an international standard on transparency and effective exchange of information. Much progress has been made and, in 2009, the last three jurisdictions that had previously been classified as uncooperative tax havens committed to the OECD standard.

◆ The price agreed for goods or services between two connected parties is known as the transfer price. The transfer price can be manipulated in order to shift profits so that they are earned in a low tax jurisdiction, which causes an unfair division between the jurisdictions and is known as the transfer pricing problem.

Part Four

Banking

After studying this part, students will gain an understanding of the banking services provided from within offshore centres. Students will be able to discuss the reasons for using offshore bank accounts, how to choose an offshore bank and explain the main disadvantage of banking offshore – that is, the lack of depositor compensation schemes. Students will be able to discuss the process of choosing, opening and closing a bank account, and will gain an understanding of various payment methods and the roles of various important bodies in the payments industry. Students will gain an understanding of the regulation and supervision of offshore banks, and the role of the Basel Committee on banking supervision. Students will gain an understanding of the banking secrecy provisions in offshore centres.

Learning outcomes

At the end of this chapter, students will be able to:

◆ discuss various types of bank accounts available;

◆ explain what the process of opening a bank account may include;

◆ discuss the process of choosing a bank account;

◆ explain what the process of closing a bank account may include;

◆ discuss different payment methods including cash, cheques, banker's drafts, BACS, CHAPS, Faster Payments, direct debits, direct credits, standing orders and bank cards;

◆ discuss the various payment systems including BACS, CHAPS, the cheque clearing system, SWIFT and SEPA;

◆ outline the roles of the cheque and credit clearing company, the Payments Council and UK Payments Administration Limited;

◆ discuss the reasons for using offshore bank accounts;

◆ discuss the disadvantages of using an offshore bank account;

◆ discuss considerations when choosing an offshore bank;

◆ discuss the banking services provided from offshore centres including foreign exchange contracts and forward exchange contracts, and the risk involved therein;

◆ discuss the regulation and supervision of offshore banks;

◆ discuss the role of the Basel Committee on banking supervision;

◆ discuss the concept of 'managed banks'; and

◆ discuss banking secrecy provisions in offshore centres.

Chapter seven
Accounts and payments

List of topics

1. Types of bank accounts
2. Opening bank accounts
3. Closing the bank accounts
4. Payment methods
5. Payment systems
6. Payment industry bodies and other organisations

Introduction

This chapter describes basic bank accounts, current accounts and savings accounts (including fixed term deposits) that are available, and describes their differences and main features. The steps involved in choosing and opening a bank account are outlined. Various payment methods such as cheques, banker's drafts, the use of bank cards and automated payments such as direct debits and standing orders are described. Payment systems including BACS, Faster Payments and CHAPS are discussed, as is the SWIFT messaging system and the cheque clearing system. Finally, the chapter explains the role of various bodies and organisations that play an important part in the payments industry including the Payments Council, UK Payments Administration Limited and the Cheque and Credit Clearing Company.

1. Types of bank accounts

Banks offer a range of different types of bank accounts with different features. The terms and conditions of similar types of account will vary from bank to bank.

1.1 Basic bank accounts

Basic bank accounts offer a convenient place to keep money to meet day-to-day expenditure.

Basic bank accounts offer some of the features that current accounts provide; however, the customer is not usually issued with a cheque book and does not have the ability to go overdrawn if there are insufficient funds available within the account. This inability to go overdrawn is an attraction for some people.

Some basic bank accounts also offer debit cards. It is possible to receive funds directly into a basic bank account and they can be used to set up direct debits or standing orders.

1.2 Current accounts

Current accounts (also known as cheque accounts) are very popular. They have more features than basic bank accounts. For example, they usually offer:

◆ a cheque book (and historically a cheque guarantee card);

◆ a debit card;

◆ direct debits;

◆ standing orders;

◆ the facility to receive Bankers' Automated Clearing Services (BACS) payments directly into the account;

◆ the facility to make BACS payments to others from the account;

◆ an overdraft facility;

◆ access to automated teller machine (ATM) facilities using a debit card; and

◆ telephone or internet banking facilities.

Customers may withdraw money on demand by using the above services and may also withdraw cash at the counter.

Historically, current accounts did not earn interest; however, this is no longer the case. Very often interest is now earned, albeit at a very low rate. The interest rates on current accounts may be tiered so that the higher the balance, the higher the interest rate earned.

The advantages to the bank of having current account holders are as follows.

◆ The customers are more likely than others to use other bank services, providing an income to the bank (e.g. overdraft charges).

◆ The more services the customer uses, the more income they generate for the bank in interest and transaction charges.

Source of funds
Activities which generate funds for a relationship.

◆ Current account balances provide a cheap **source of funds** for banks as they can lend these balances and receive more interest than they pay on the current accounts.

1.3 Savings accounts

Savings accounts are suitable for customers who seek a return on their savings while keeping their savings in a safe, accessible place.

Banks offer a range of different types of savings accounts with different features. The following are types of savings accounts that are available.

Fixed term deposits

A fixed term deposit involves the customer agreeing to deposit a sum of money with the bank for a specified period of time. Some banks impose a minimum balance requirement. Fixed terms could range from daily to weekly or monthly, or could even be fixed for one year or more.

As the deposit is 'fixed' and no withdrawals or additions are anticipated, the account does not offer the payment facilities that are available on, for example, a current account.

Usually, the interest rates paid on a fixed deposit increase the longer the funds are committed and the interest is applied to the account at the end of the term. The bank can offer a better rate of interest as it knows that it has use of the money for a specified period. Fixed term deposits do not usually allow for part withdrawals. Penalties for breaking a fixed deposit are usually severe and a customer must therefore ensure that they will not require access to the funds during the term. Trust and company administrators should be conscious of any liquidity requirements (such as the need to have funds available to settle liabilities such as trustee fees) when fixing or re-fixing deposits at their maturity.

Instant access accounts

Instant access accounts may require a large initial investment. The interest rate payable is usually preferable and tiered in accordance with the level of funds in the account.

These accounts allow instant access to funds without the loss of interest. The terms of instant access accounts may provide that no interest will be payable if the balance of the accounts falls below a minimum – for example, £5,000.

Other savings accounts

The terms and features of savings accounts available differ from bank to bank.

Some accounts allow funds to be withdrawn on demand with instant access, while others require the customer to give the bank notice before funds can be withdrawn. The notice period can vary from one week to, for example, three months.

Some savings accounts require regular savings of a minimum savings amount each month while others are suitable for those with a large lump sum.

Interest at varying frequencies may be applied to savings accounts on, for example, a monthly or six-monthly basis.

Test yourself 7.1

Distinguish between a fixed term deposit account and a current account.

1.4 Sharia accounts

Sharia-compliant bank accounts are designed and run in accordance with Islamic laws. They offer features similar to other kinds of accounts but do not pay interest or charge interest on the bank account. In addition, the bank usually undertakes not to invest the customer's money in interest-based activities. They do not usually allow an account to go overdrawn. Such accounts are usually supervised by Islamic scholars who ensure that the account is operated in accordance with Islamic law and finance.

2. Opening bank accounts

The following steps are involved in opening a bank account.

◆ The customer chooses the type of account required.

◆ The customer completes an application form.

◆ The customer provides the bank with any due diligence documentation that it may require in order to prove the identity of the customer. This commonly involves providing the bank with a certified copy of a document (e.g. a passport) which verifies the customer's identity, a certified copy of the utility bill which verifies the customer's residential (or registered office) address and providing a recent bank statement that verifies the customer's wealth or earnings.

◆ The account is funded.

Corporate applicants may be asked to provide due diligence documentation in respect of their controllers (e.g. the directors and controlling shareholders) or other account signatories and may be requested to provide additional documentation in relation to the legal person (the company) including certified copies of:

◆ the memorandum and articles of association;

◆ the Certificate of Incorporation;

◆ a Certificate of 'Good Standing' issued by the Companies Registry (or a resident agent in some jurisdictions);

◆ a copy of the board resolution authorising the opening of the bank account documentation to be signed;

◆ a copy of the register of members;

◆ a copy of the register of directors and secretaries; and

◆ a copy of the signatory list of the company.

Trustees who wish to open trust bank accounts may be requested to provide documentation containing details of:

◆ the trust (e.g. the name and type of trust and trustees);

◆ the settlor;

◆ the principal beneficiaries; and

◆ any protector.

Corporate trustees may be asked to provide additional information in line with that of corporate applicants.

In all cases, the rationale for the opening of the bank account, the activity of the entity, the source of funds, **source of wealth** and expected volume and value of transactions are likely to be requested.

Banks often try to identify accounts which may present higher risks to them and may therefore ask questions such as whether or not a politically exposed person is connected to the account or whether the funds in the account are received as a result of consultancy fees or commissions.

Source of wealth
Activities which have generated the total net worth of a person.

2.1 Bank mandates

When a new account is opened, the customer signs a mandate which often forms a part of the account opening documentation. The mandate appoints the bank as the customer's banker and authorises it to open the bank account.

The mandate also:

◆ authorises the bank to honour all cheques drawn on the account;

◆ authorises the bank to accept and act on all instructions in relation to the account (including payment instructions);

◆ sets out the signing authorities that the bank should accept instructions from. Offshore trust and company businesses may have an authorised signatory list that includes their staff members and it is common for them to complete this section of the mandate with a statement which authorises the bank to accept instructions where they are signed 'in accordance with the global signatory list of (e.g. the trust company) as amended from time to time'; and

◆ sets out that the bank may allow the account to go overdrawn if it acts on the customer's instructions.

2.2 Facsimile indemnity

Where a customer wishes to communicate with a bank by facsimile, the bank may insist upon receiving an indemnity which absolves the bank from all responsibility, and releases it from claims and demands that the bank may incur due to it having acted on faxed instructions and indemnifies the bank against liability and loss as a result of having honoured a faxed instruction.

2.3 Choosing a bank account

The following are considerations that may be relevant when choosing a bank account:

◆ the charges to be applied to the account;

◆ the rate of interest to be credited to the account;

◆ whether interest is paid gross of tax;

◆ the choice of currencies;

◆ 24-hour banking facilities;

◆   internet and telephone banking facilities;

◆   international money transfers;

◆   the account opening fee or any ongoing monthly fee;

◆   accessibility of the funds (i.e. any notice requirement and low penalties);

◆   minimum balance requirements;

◆   the charges to be applied to the account;

◆   compensation arrangements; and

◆   whether the account is Sharia-compliant.

Some banks aim their accounts at particular types of customers and may therefore refuse to open an account for someone who does not meet the criteria for a particular account (e.g. a requirement for the customer to earn a certain level of salary).

3. Closing the bank accounts

It is usually possible to close a bank account at any time without charge or penalty. Some accounts may have conditions upon closing the account – for example, fixed term deposits – however, any such conditions must be made clear to the customer before the account is opened.

The bank or building society may decide to close a bank account. The bank should give 'reasonable notice' to enable its customer to make other arrangements. What is considered reasonable will differ from account to account.

Stop and think 7.1

It is good practice to ensure that trust and company administrators properly close the bank accounts of client entities (i.e. trusts or companies under administration) when they are no longer required or at the end of the business relationship. Dormant accounts that are not monitored present risks to the service provider; for example, unexpected receipts may arrive in the account and remain unnoticed. This leaves the trust company unable to perform the required due diligence in respect of the source of funds in breach of AML/CFT legislation and exposes the company to the risk of theft by its employees.

4. Payment methods

4.1 Cash

Cash is used for many everyday small transactions and is a very convenient payment method. Cash is a trusted method of payment. Cash is available on demand by customers with access to ATMs.

Prior to the introduction of legislation on the proceeds of crime, customers could visit their bankers in offshore centres and deposit or leave with large sums of cash. This practice is no longer prevalent in well-regulated jurisdictions.

4.2 Cheques

A cheque is a written instruction from an account holder to their bank to pay a specified sum of money to a named beneficiary (a payee).

Cheques are usually written on a standard form provided by the bank in a cheque book. The standard form is a slip which contains pre-printed information such as the branch of the bank on which the cheque is drawn, the sort code number of the branch on which the cheque is drawn, the account number and the name of the drawer (the writer) of the cheque.

The cheque number, the sort code and account number is included at the bottom of each pre-printed cheque in ink that can be read electronically when the cheque passes through the general cheque clearing system. The general cheque clearing system is discussed in section 5.6 of this chapter.

The customer completes the cheque by hand when they wish to make an instruction to pay a beneficiary by completing the name of the payee, the amount of the payment in words and numbers, and signs and dates the cheque.

The use of cheques has been in decline for several years as electronic methods of payment have become more popular. It was for this reason, in December 2009, that the Payments Council set a target date for closing the general cheque clearing system by October 2018. The Payments Council announced that a decision to continue with the closing of the general cheque clearing system would be made in 2016 as long as viable alternatives to cheques had been put in place.

Many stakeholder groups including charities and pensioner lobby groups objected to the closure of the general cheque clearing system. In July 2011, the Payments Council announced that, having listened to stakeholders, it had decided that the cheque would stay and that the 2018 target date had been withdrawn.

In offshore centres, cheques are seen as a convenient and cost-effective way for companies (particularly property holding companies) to settle invoices including property maintenance expenses and they are often used for this purpose.

4.3 Banker's drafts

Banker's drafts are cheques drawn directly on the account of the bank rather than the account of the customer.

Before a person can request their bank to issue a banker's draft, they are required to have cleared funds available in their account in order to cover the amount of the draft. The customer's account is then immediately debited with the amount of the draft and the bank's own account credited. The funds remain on the bank's account until the draft is presented by the payee and cleared.

As banker's drafts are drawn on the account of the bank, they provide additional comfort to the payee that they are unlikely to be returned unpaid due to a lack of funds. Banker's drafts were often used for transactions involving large amounts of money where the payee wished to eliminate the risk of the cheque bouncing. They do not, however, provide a guarantee against fraudulent use.

4.4 Bank cards

Cheque guarantee cards

Cheque guarantee cards could be used when paying to guarantee a cheque for amounts up to £250. For a cheque to be guaranteed, a cheque guarantee card would have to be handed over with it and the rules of the scheme complied with. As the use of cheques has declined over the years, so has the use of cheque guarantee cards.

The Payments Council which sets the strategy for payments in the UK decided that as the use of cheque guarantee cards was in decline, it would set a closure date for the scheme and as a result the facility to guarantee a cheque using a plastic card was withdrawn on 30 June 2011.

Debit cards

Debit cards are plastic cards that allow a customer to pay for goods and services and have largely replaced the need for people to write cheques. The card sends an instruction to the cardholder's bank to debit their account and credit the payee's account for the cost of the goods or services.

Debit cards can be used at ATM machines (discussed later in this section) to withdraw cash or access other bank services, and can be used to purchase goods by telephone and over the internet.

At the point of payment (when used in person), the cardholder hands their card to the salesperson, who will ask the cardholder to key into a special machine their private personal identification number (PIN).

Prior to the introduction of PINs, the retailer would have asked the cardholder to sign a sales voucher. However, from February 2006, cardholders have been required to use their PIN as without it, their card may be declined. Since 1 January 2005, if the use of a Chip and PIN device could have prevented a fraud and a retailer does not use one, the retailer may bear the cost of the fraudulent transaction. Prior to this date, the UK card issuers suffered the cost of any fraud. The change in liability to the retailers was referred to as 'the liability shift'.

Credit cards

Credit cards can be used in the same way as debit cards to pay for goods and services; however, they differ from debit cards as the cost of the goods or service is not taken directly from the cardholder's bank account. Instead, the card funds up to a personal spending limit which varies from cardholder to cardholder and from bank to bank. The amount of the personal spending limit is made available to the customer by the bank. The cardholder can use the credit card to access these funds directly from the bank when purchasing goods and services.

The cardholder can then choose how much to repay the bank each month, subject usually to a minimum amount (which could be as low as £5). The cardholder could repay the balance in full if they chose to do so. The customer could pay their chosen amount each month using a range of payment methods including cash or direct debit.

Any unpaid balance on the credit card incurs interest, usually at a very high rate.

Stop and think 7.2

Some offshore service providers have issued their clients with credit cards that are drawn on the account of the trust or an underlying company. Consider the trustee issues, the management and control issues, and the AML issues that could arise as a result of this practice.

Automated teller machine (ATM) cards

An ATM is a machine that can be located outside a bank (e.g. within a shop or the high street) which enables customers to gain access 24 hours a day, seven days a week to some banking services. While the services differ from bank to bank, they may include:

◆   cash withdrawals (usually limited e.g. to £250 per day);

◆   the viewing of the account balance;

◆   ordering a bank statement;

◆   ordering a cheque book;

◆   paying in cheques; and

◆   obtaining a mini statement listing the last few transactions on the account.

The customer accesses the services by inserting their ATM card into the machine and entering in their PIN. Debit cards and credit cards can usually be used at an ATM.

Internet and telephone

Internet or telephone transactions are either processed using the faster payments service or by using the BACS system. The BACS system is discussed further in section 5 of this chapter.

4.5 Automated payments

Direct debits

A direct debit is an instruction from a customer to their bank authorising an organisation to collect varying amounts from their bank accounts, as long as the customer has been given advance notice of the collection amounts and dates. The bank then simply allows the money to be taken from the account.

Direct debits are an extremely convenient way to pay household bills or other regular invoices where the amount varies as there is no need to inform the bank that the amount has changed, as would be required if the bills were settled by standing order. Direct debits are settled via the BACS system.

Direct credits

A direct credit enables organisations to make payments by electronic transfer directly into bank accounts.

Direct credit is mainly used for paying wages and salaries. Organisations may also use direct credits for supplier payments, pensions, employee expenses, insurance settlements and dividends.

Standing orders

A standing order is an instruction to a bank to make payments for a fixed amount to the same beneficiary at a UK bank or building society account on a regular basis – for example, every month on a particular date during the month. Any person with a current account at a bank in the UK can set up a standing order.

Online banking has made it extremely easy for customers who have access to the online banking facility to set up standing orders with some banks online. They can also be set up after the customer has completed a pre-printed form that includes the details that the bank requires. The bank then follows the customer's instructions and continues to make the payments until the customer cancels the standing order or a specified final payment date is reached.

The funds will be transferred either through the BACS system or through the faster payments service. Funds transferred through the BACS system will be received by the recipient within three working days and funds transferred through the faster payment system will be processed on the same day.

International Bank Account Numbers

International bank account numbers (IBANs) were introduced to help speed up international payments by standardising the identification of bank accounts and thereby reducing errors and delays. To make a European cross-border payment, customers need to quote an IBAN and its associated Bank Identification Code (BIC).

The IBAN is comprised of the country code (two digits) and a two-digit check number, the first four characters of the BIC, the sort code and the account number.

Test yourself 7.2

Outline six methods of withdrawing funds from a bank account.

---

5. Payment systems

5.1 BACS

BACS is a not-for-profit, membership-based industry body that is owned by 15 of the leading banks and building societies in the UK and Europe.

BACS is responsible for the schemes behind the clearing and settlement of automated payments in the UK, including direct debits, and BACS direct credit.

5.2 Faster payments

The Faster Payments Service is the first new payment service to be introduced in the UK for more than 20 years. Thirteen banks and building societies were founding members of the new service and other financial institutions are able to join as members or to access the system through agency arrangements with a member, as they do with other payment systems.

UK Payments Administration Limited started the Faster Payments Service initiative to improve the speed of lower transactions, to be used in parallel with the CHAPS and BACS systems. The Faster Payments Service enables telephone, internet and standing order payments to move within a few hours, almost at the touch of a button. As it operates in near real time, payments made via the Faster Payments Service cannot be recalled.

The Faster Payments Service can be used to make one-off payments or standing orders in sterling. Direct debits are not a part of the service.

5.3 CHAPS

The Clearing House Automated Payment System (also known as CHAPS) is a British company which was established in 1984. CHAPS offers same-day sterling fund transfers. It used to offer euro funds transfers; however this service is now closed.

A CHAPS transfer is initiated by the customer to move money to a recipient's bank account at another bank, where the funds need to be cleared (made available) the same working day.

Unlike a bank giro credit, a pre-printed slip specifying the recipient's details is not required. Unlike cheques, the funds transfer is performed in real time and is irrevocable. This removes the potential for payments to be stopped by the sender, or returns due to insufficient funds even after they appear to have arrived in the destination account, a problem which can be experienced with other payment methods such as cheques.

CHAPS is a real time, gross settlement (RTGS) system. RTGS is the continuous settlement of funds or securities transfers on an order-by-order basis (without netting).

5.4 The Society for Worldwide Interbank Financial Telecommunication (SWIFT)

SWIFT is a member-owned cooperative society under Belgian law. Twenty-five independent directors govern and oversee its management. From 1998, oversight of SWIFT has been by the central banks of the G10 countries.

In 1973, SWIFT, supported by 239 banks in 15 countries, started the creation of a shared data processing and communications language for international financial transactions. At the time that SWIFT went live in 1977, there were 518 members (who were commercial banks) in 22 countries. In 2008, there were 8,468 users in 208 countries.

SWIFT is neither a payment nor a settlement system; however, a number of payment systems depend on SWIFT.

SWIFT operates a network which facilitates the exchange of messages (including payment messages) between financial institutions. A SWIFT payment message is an instruction to transfer funds. The settlement then takes place via a payment system.

Users of SWIFT are able to develop internal applications which link into the SWIFT network via computer terminals which meet SWIFT specifications. These terminals can then be used to allow transactions to be processed without the need for the information to be re-input manually.

Messages formatted using SWIFT standards can be read and processed by many payment systems. SWIFT cooperates with international organisations such as the ISO (the International Organization for Standardization) in order to define standards for message format and content.

Users of SWIFT include its shareholders (members such as banks, eligible securities broker dealers and regulated investment management institutions), organisations that meet the criteria to be members (but are not members) and sub-members (organisations that are owned and controlled by shareholders).

5.5 Single European Payments Area (SEPA)

The SEPA programme is an initiative of the European Payments Council that brings together the European payments industry.

The SEPA is the area where participants can make and receive payments in euros, within Europe under the same basic conditions, regardless of the national boundaries (i.e. all euro payments will be considered to be domestic). SEPA aims to achieve faster settlement and simplified processing, improving cash flow while reducing costs.

5.6 The cheque clearing system

As explained above, a cheque is a written order to pay a specified sum from an account (the drawer's account) to that of the beneficiary (the payee).

After the cheque is passed to the payee, the process is as follows.

- The payee sends the cheque to their bank.
- The payee's bank then sends the cheque to central clearing.
- Central clearing then forwards it to the main clearing department of the drawer's bank (not the drawer's own branch).
- The clearing department of the bank then sends the cheque to the branch at which the bank account is held.
- If funds are available, the cheque will be cleared for payment by the drawer's branch.
- If there are insufficient funds to clear the cheque, the cheque is returned unpaid. Unpaid cheques are usually returned on the same day that the paying banker receives them.

It is possible for cheques to be sent for direct clearance or presentation. In these circumstances, the payee's bank sends the cheque by post to the paying banker. The next morning, the collecting banker (the payee's banker) telephones the paying banker and receives confirmation over the telephone as to whether or not the cheque has been paid. A fee is charged for this service.

In November 2007, changes to the cheque clearing cycle known as the 2-4-6 and the 2-6-6 cheque clearing timescales changes came into force, giving customers increased clarity and certainty with regards to the timescale involved in the clearing of the cheque.

The 2-4-6 timescale for the clearing of the cheques paid into current accounts means that:

- the process starts when the cheque is received by the payee's bank;
- no later than two days after this, the payee starts to receive interest on the money (i.e. the second business day after paying in the cheque);
- no later than four days after the cheque was received by the payee's bank, the bank will allow the payee to withdraw the funds (i.e. the fourth business day after paying in the cheque); and
- by the end of six days, the payee can be certain that the cheque will not bounce and that the money cannot be reclaimed from their account without their consent (i.e. the sixth business day).

For savings accounts, the maximum time limit for withdrawal is longer (six days) and is known as 2-6-6.

The clearing system does not operate on Saturdays, Sundays or bank holidays.

Test yourself 7.3

If a cheque was paid into a savings account on a Monday, on what day would the bank allow the payee to withdraw the funds?

6. Payment industry bodies and other organisations

6.1 The Payments Council

The Payments Council is a voluntary membership organisation which is funded by its members. It is governed by a set of published rules and a board of directors. Organisations that are payment service providers with qualifying payment volumes can join the Payments Council.

The principal UK payment schemes such as BACS, CHAPS, the Cheque and Credit Clearing Company Limited, the UK Domestic Cheque Guarantee Card Scheme and the LINK ATM scheme have all entered into a contract with the Payments Council.

The board of the Payments Council will consult on important issues such as proposals for innovation, any significant policy statements and any proposals to create wind-down payment systems in the UK.

The Payments Council is the organisation that sets the strategy for UK payments. It has been established to ensure that UK payment systems and services meet the needs of users, payment service providers and the wider economy.

The Payments Council has three core objectives.

1. to have a strategic vision for payments and lead the future development of cooperative payment services in the UK;
2. to ensure payment systems are open, accountable and transparent; and
3. to ensure the operational efficiency, effectiveness and integrity of payment services in the UK.

Each scheme has entered into a contract or other formal arrangement with the Payments Council to set up their respective rights and duties towards each other.

Under the contracts, schemes are required to report to the board of the Payments Council. The board is also able to make decisions that are binding on scheme members in order to implement its strategy.

6.2 UK Payments Administration Limited

UK Payments Administration Limited, previously known as APACS (Association for Payment Clearing Services) is a UK trade organisation.

UK Payments Administration Limited provide services to a wide range of companies including:

◆ BACS;
◆ CHAPS;
◆ Cheque and Credit Clearing Company;

◆   Faster Payments;

◆   Payments Council; and

◆   Swift UK.

The organisation covers most forms of payments within the UK including cash, credit cards, debit cards, cheques and automated payments such as direct debits.

The role of UK Payments Administration Limited is:

◆   to develop and support the development of appropriate national and international standards for the payments industry; and

◆   to coordinate UK payments standards activities of behalf of the Payments Council, interest groups and the clearing companies, ensuring that there is clear and consistent policy and business rationale wherever possible, and in doing so provide a centre of expertise.

UK Payments Administration Limited brings together all payment systems organisations and gives banks, building societies and card issuers the forum where they can work together on non-competitive issues. It was responsible for the creation of rules regarding customer liability in cases of card and cheque fraud, and recently oversaw and guided the transition of debit cards to Chip and PIN.

The Standards Policy Group of UK Payments Administration Limited reports directly to the Payments Council board and it is responsible for setting policy and strategic direction and standards at the Payments Council.

UK Payments Administration Limited works closely with industry bodies associated with standards. One such body is the International Organization for Standardization (ISO).

Test yourself 7.4

Outline the role of UK Payments Administration Limited within the payments industry.

6.3 The International Organization for Standardization

The International Organization for Standardization (ISO) is the world's largest developer and publisher of international standards. The ISO is a non-governmental organisation.

The ISO is a network of the national standards Institute of 157 countries, one member per country, with a central secretariat in Geneva that coordinates the system.

6.4 The Cheque and Credit Clearing Company

The Cheque and Credit Clearing Company is a membership-based non-profit-making industry body which manages the cheque clearing system in Great Britain.

As well as clearing cheques, the system processes banker's drafts, building society cheques, postal orders and traveller's cheques.

The Cheque and Credit Clearing Company also manages the system for the clearing of paperback giro credits (credit clearing), euro cheques (euro clearing) and US dollar cheques (the currency clearing the US dollar cheques drawn on Great Britain accounts).

The Cheque and Credit Clearing Company describes its role as being to:

◆ provide members with the central infrastructure for the exchange and settlement of cheques and credits (i.e. the exchange centres, the network for the transfer of electronic cheque data, an automated settlement system), and the courier service for the return of unpaid cheques to the collecting bank;

◆ manage the operational processes of the central infrastructure;

◆ determine the rules, standards and procedures required to maintain the integrity of the clearings, including the criteria for joining the clearings;

◆ ensure that members comply with the rules, standards and procedures;

◆ provide thought leadership in non-competitive matters relating to cheques and cheque clearing;

◆ engage with the full range of stakeholders, from cheque users, to banks that offer cheque clearing services, to the cheque processes, to cheque printers and suppliers of all kinds, and to regulators, trade associations and other payment schemes; and

◆ manage the Cheque Printer Accreditation Scheme.

Chapter summary

◆ There are different types of bank accounts such as basic bank accounts, current accounts and savings accounts which include fixed term deposit accounts.

◆ Current accounts allow customers to withdraw funds on demand and pay low rates of interest, whereas savings accounts usually require notice before funds can be withdrawn and usually offer higher rates of interest.

◆ Banks offer a range of different types of savings accounts with different features and the terms and conditions of similar types of accounts will vary from bank to bank. Some may aim their accounts at particular types of customers and may therefore refuse to open an account for someone who does not meet the criteria for a particular account.

◆ It is usually possible for the customer to close a bank account at any time without charge although some accounts (e.g. fixed term deposits) may have conditions upon closing the account. If the bank decides to close a bank account, it should give reasonable notice to the customer.

◆ Cash, cheques, banker's drafts, the use of bank cards such as credit or debit cards and automated payments such as direct debits or standing orders are all payment methods which are useful in different circumstances.

◆ Payment systems include BACS, Faster Payments, CHAPS and the cheque clearing system. The SWIFT messaging system is also an important.

◆ The Payments Council, UK Payments Administration Limited and the Cheque and Credit Clearing Company are all important industry bodies in the UK payments industry.

Chapter eight
Offshore banking services

List of topics

1. Banking business
2. Banking services provided from offshore centres
3. Regulation and supervision of offshore banking
4. Obtaining a banking licence
5. Managed banks
6. Banking secrecy laws

Introduction

This chapter outlines the main reasons why a customer may wish to open an offshore bank account and the main reasons that a bank may wish to offer services from an offshore location. This chapter discusses various factors that a customer may wish to consider when choosing to use an offshore bank and explains the main downfall of offshore banking: the lack of depositor compensation schemes. Banking services provided from offshore centres are outlined including the foreign exchange market and forward exchange contracts. The issue of regulation and supervision of offshore banks is discussed and the international standards set by the Basel Committee are discussed, as is the issue of banking secrecy laws that are present in some offshore centres. The savings directive is also discussed and the advantages of managed banks are outlined.

1. Banking business

Offshore banking is simply having a bank account outside of your country of residence. It is very common for banks in offshore centres to be locally incorporated subsidiaries of large onshore banking groups that wish to provide the offshore banking facility to existing clients and others are branches of mainland banks.

The banking industry in offshore centres is often complementary to other parts of their finance sector. It supports the trust and fiduciary sector by providing a range of services, including the taking of deposits, to the structures established within the offshore centre. The banking industry also supports the collective investment fund sector by providing overdraft and liquidity facilities to funds to enable them to finance the timing differences between the purchase and sale of securities and the flows of subscriptions and redemptions by investors and by taking deposits from the uninvested balances of fund administration companies. Insurance sectors may be supported by the provision of standby letters of credit to captive insurance companies.

Banks accept deposits from customers, often on a short-term basis, and lend to other customers, sometimes for longer periods – for example, as would be required with a mortgage. Offshore centres are sometimes in the position where the level of deposits they receive outweighs the borrowing needs of local customers. The banks therefore lend the majority of their deposits to parent banks or group companies. Banks in offshore centres are therefore valuable suppliers of funding and liquidity to mainland banks.

1.1 Reasons for using an offshore bank account

The main reasons why a customer may wish to open an offshore bank account include the following.

◆ Interest is usually paid gross (i.e. it is unlikely that any tax will be deducted at source on interest earned). Residents in the EU will, however, be subject to the European Savings Tax Directive which is discussed in section 8 of Chapter 5.

◆ Depending on where the client is resident, offshore income may not be subject to tax in their country of residence if the income is not remitted back to that country.

◆ Offshore centres often benefit from statutory secrecy or confidentiality provisions that enhance the normal common law principles that apply to the customer/banker relationship.

◆ In some offshore centres, less stringent regulation and supervision could reduce the bank's costs and enable a higher rate of interest to be paid to customers.

A bank may wish to offer services from an offshore location because:

◆ the tax liability on profits arising may be low;

◆ there is less stringent regulation and supervision;

◆ costs for premises and staff may be lower; and

◆ it wishes to complement the services that it can provide to its client base (i.e. to provide offshore products and services).

Test yourself 8.1

Outline three reasons why a customer may choose to open an offshore bank account.

1.2 Considerations when choosing to use a bank located in an offshore centre

The following are considerations that may be relevant when choosing to use a bank in an offshore centre:

- the quality of the banks operating within the offshore centre;
- the regulatory requirements and the effectiveness of the regulatory oversight;
- the absence of bank failures; and
- the availability of a depositor compensation scheme.

1.3 Depositor compensation schemes

In the past it has been uncommon for offshore centres to have depositor compensation schemes. For example, until recently Jersey and Guernsey had no depositor compensation scheme at all, and until recently, in the Isle of Man, only 75% of the first £25,000 was protected.

The global crisis, however, and in particular reports of bank failures in some jurisdictions has caused offshore centres to introduce depositor compensation schemes in order to give comfort to offshore investors. Jersey, for example, introduced a depositor compensation scheme in November 2009 that would protect deposits of up to £50,000 in the event of a Jersey bank failing. Guernsey introduced its compensation scheme in November 2008 and also guarantees deposits of up to £50,000. The Isle of Man scheme is now in line with that of Jersey and Guernsey.

It is common for the benefits of such schemes to be available to private individuals (i.e. retail deposits) and charities only, and to provide protection for deposits of up to a certain amount, for example, £50,000, in the event of the offshore bank failing. Depositor protection does not typically extend to corporations, partnerships or trusts. The Isle of Man scheme, however, protects non-individuals (i.e. trusts, charities and businesses) up to a maximum of £20,000.

The majority of the cost of the compensation schemes is usually borne by the banking industry.

Making it work 8.1: The collapse of Landsbanki Guernsey Limited

In 2008, Landsbanki Guernsey Limited went into voluntary administration. Its customers were not covered by the UK or the Icelandic protection schemes because the bank was a Guernsey company and at the time, Guernsey did not have a depositor compensation scheme in place.

Immediately after the collapse of Landsbanki Guernsey Limited, the Guernsey government introduced a depositor compensation scheme, although this excluded the Landsbanki Guernsey customers.

Landsbanki customers in the UK and the Netherlands received 100% of their deposits much sooner than the Guernsey customers due to the depositor compensation schemes available in their jurisdiction. Customers of Landsbanki Guernsey (a third of whom were expatriates) eventually received approximately 67.5p for every £1 that they had deposited.

2. Banking services provided from offshore centres

The services provided and terms and conditions will vary from bank to bank.

Offshore banks provide usual banking services such as:

◆ current accounts;
◆ overdraft facilities;
◆ deposit and savings accounts;
◆ mortgage facilities;
◆ lending facilities;
◆ payments facilities, including online banking and telephone banking;
◆ debit cards and credit cards and cheque books;
◆ foreign exchange; and
◆ forward exchange contracts.

2.1 The foreign exchange markets

Foreign exchange is a service that is often offered by banks both onshore and offshore. Banks buy currency from and sell foreign currency to customers on the foreign exchange market.

The foreign exchange market is sometimes referred to as the forex market, the FX market or the currency market. The foreign exchange market is a decentralised global marketplace.

Some banks offer foreign exchange services by telephone or online banking. The bank may impose transaction limits or require notice of larger foreign exchange transactions or for transactions involving certain currencies, although the terms that banks can offer will vary from bank to bank.

Foreign exchange services offered by banks range from simply informing a customer who has a foreign currency invoice to pay what the cost will be in local currency to more complex transactions such as forward exchange contracts (discussed in section 2.2 of this chapter) or by putting in place a portfolio of hedges to manage the foreign currency risk that a business may face.

Currency rates can have an effect on the cost of doing business. For example, a business that needs to pay USD10,000 to import goods to the UK would pay GBP6,141.38 if the rate was GBP1 to USD1.6283. However, if the rate changed to GBP1 to USD 1.5057, the business would have to pay GBP6,641.38 (an extra £500) in order to pay the USD10,000 price.

Banks make a profit by charging a commission on each foreign exchange deal. There is also a spread between the buying rate (the rate at which the bank will buy the currency from the customer) and the selling rate (the rate at which the bank will sell the customer the foreign currency). A spot transaction is a foreign exchange transaction that usually settles within two days. This type of transaction does not involve an ongoing contract (unlike forward exchange deals as detailed below).

2.2 Forward exchange contracts

A forward exchange contract (FEC) is a binding contract to buy or sell a given quantity of a foreign currency at a future date, at a rate of exchange that is determined when the FEC is made.

Customers may wish to enter into a FEC with a view to using the funds in the future to fulfil a business transaction on a named date. The exact terms of the contract may differ between banks; for example, some banks may offer flexibility and allow a period of time between two dates to be specified for settlement of the contract.

With an FEC, the customer pays a foreign exchange rate which is based on the spot rate on the day of the deal.

◆ With an FEC, the rate of exchange is guaranteed, enabling a business to determine in advance what its costs will be (or how much income will be received).

◆ FECs offer protection against adverse exchange rate movements in an easy and low-cost way.

◆ FECs assist a business to budget and manage future sales and invoicing.

The risk with an FEC is that if the exchange rate moves against the customer, they are still legally bound to settle at the exchange rate specified in the contract.

Test yourself 8.2

What is a forward exchange contract?

3. Regulation and supervision of offshore banking

3.1 The Group of International Finance Centre Supervisors

The Offshore Group of Banking Supervisors was formed in October 1980 at the instigation of the Basel Committee on Banking Supervision as an association of the authorities concerned with the supervision of Banks of offshore finance centres and related financial services. The group changed its name to the Group of International Finance Centre Supervisors (GIFCS) in March 2011 in order to reflect better the wider scope of its activities.

It is a condition of membership that an offshore centre must demonstrate a clear commitment to the implementation of the Core Principles set by the Basel Committee on banking supervision which sets the international standard. A jurisdiction's observance of the core principles is assessed by the International Monetary Fund (IMF).

3.2 The Basel Committee on Banking Supervision

The Basel Committee on Banking Supervision (BCBS) was established in 1974 by the Central Bank governors of the Group of 10 (G10) countries. The BCBS formulates supervisory standards and guidelines, and recommends statements of best practice which it expects member countries to implement in a way that authorities in each country sees fit. The BCBS standards or guidelines do not have legal force and it does not have any formal supervisory authority.

The functions of the BCBS are:

◆ the provision of a forum for regular cooperation on banking supervisory matters;
◆ a standard-setting body on all aspects of banking supervision;
◆ to enhance understanding of key supervisory issues; and
◆ to improve the quality of banking supervision worldwide.

The BCBS is best known for its International Standards on Capital Adequacy (the Basel Capital Accord) and the Core Principles for Effective Banking Supervision (the Core Principles).

3.3 The Basel Capital Accord

Basel I
In 1988, the Basel Committee introduced a capital measurement system which is referred to the Basel Capital Accord. The 1988 accord (known as Basel I) primarily focussed on the implementation of a credit risk management framework. The Basel I framework was revised on 26 June 2004.

Basel II

The revised capital adequacy framework is known as Basel II. The Basel II framework is documented in a paper entitled 'International Convergence of Capital Measurement and Capital Standards – A Revised Framework'.

The aim of the Basel II framework is to:

◆ strengthen further the soundness and stability of the international banking system;

◆ establish closer alignment of regulatory capital requirements with economic capital needs; and

◆ maintain sufficient consistency such that capital adequacy regulation would not be a significant cause of competitive inequality among internationally active banks.

The regulators in Jersey, Guernsey and the Isle of Man worked together as a 'Tri-Party Group' in order to harmonise (wherever possible) their approaches to the implementation of Basel II.

By doing so, the regulators hoped to make it easier for those banks which operate in all three jurisdictions and avoid the potential for regulatory arbitrage.

Basel II uses a three-pillar approach. The 'Three Pillars' of Basel II cover:

◆ minimum capital requirements, which refined the standardised rules of the 1988 accord;

◆ supervisory review of an institution's internal assessment process and capital adequacy; and

◆ effective use of disclosure to strengthen market discipline as a complement to supervisory efforts.

On 4 July 2006, the BCBS issued a comprehensive version of the Basel II framework that was a compilation of the June 2004 framework, various amendments that had been made to the 1998 capital accord and a November 2005 guidance paper on the application of Basel II in certain circumstances. It did not introduce any new elements and was issued purely as a matter of convenience to readers.

Basel III

In response to the financial crisis of 2008, the Committee has developed new global standards to address both firm-specific and broader systemic risks. The revised standards have been referred to as Basel III. This builds on 'The International Convergence of Capital Measurement and Capital Standards document' (Basel II) and is a comprehensive set of reform measures to strengthen regulation, supervision and risk management of the banking sector. The new standards were announced on 12 September 2010.

3.4 The Basel Committee's Core Principles for Effective Banking Supervision

In September 1997, the BCBS published the 'Core Principles for Effective Banking Supervision' (the Core Principles). The BCBS describes the Core Principles as a comprehensive blueprint for an effective supervisory system. In order to facilitate implementation and assessment, the BCBS developed the 'Core Principles Methodology' in 1999. The most recent revision of these two documents was released in October 2006.

The Core Principles are a voluntary framework of minimum standards for sound and effective banking supervisory practices which are designed to be applied by all countries in the supervision of the banks in their jurisdiction. While they are considered to be universally applicable, national authorities may put in place supplementary measures in order to achieve effective supervision in their own jurisdictions as they see fit.

The Core Principles are categorised into seven groups covering:

1. objectives, independence, powers, transparency and cooperation (Principle 1);
2. licensing and structure (Principles 2–5);
3. prudential regulation and requirements (Principles 6–18);
4. methods of ongoing banking supervision (Principles 19–21);
5. accounting and disclosure (Principle 22);
6. corrective and remedial powers of supervisors (Principle 23); and
7. consolidated and cross-border banking supervision (Principles 24 and 25).

Preconditions for effective banking supervision

The Core Principles for effective banking supervision paper states that an effective system of banking supervision needs to be based on a number of external elements or preconditions. These include:

◆ sound and sustainable macroeconomic policies;
◆ a well-developed public infrastructure;
◆ effective market discipline; and
◆ mechanisms for providing an appropriate level of systemic protection (or public safety net).

Test yourself 8.3

State the four preconditions that are required for an effective system of banking supervision according to the Core Principles for Effective Banking Supervision paper.

4. Obtaining a banking licence

Before a bank is permitted to undertake deposit-taking business from within an offshore centre, it is required to obtain a licence from its regulator to do so. The regulator may be known as a 'financial services commission'. The requirement to obtain a licence will be set out in the offshore centre's primary legislation, which usually makes it an offence to conduct such business without a licence.

Each offshore centre will have its own licensing policy or set criteria which it uses to determine the eligibility of a bank to operate in its jurisdiction. Jersey, for example, has a strict requirement for the bank to be a member of the top 500 banks in the world, measured by Tier 1 capital size. Other offshore centres do not impose such a requirement.

Some offshore centres have one all-encompassing category of banking licence while others have various levels of licensing where the banking business that they undertake may be restricted.

When issuing a banking licence, the regulator in an offshore centre will undertake a fit and proper assessment of the applicant in order to decide whether or not the applicant should be granted a licence to undertake banking business in their jurisdiction. They may assess the following.

◆ The track record of the applicant as a banking business – for example, whether it has been supervised by a relevant authority, its audit history, the stability of its management team, whether it conducts its business with integrity and has due regard for the interests of its customers. The regulator will also consider the risk profile of the applicant including the nature of activities that it will provide and its intended customer base and target markets.

◆ The stature of the applicant. The regulator will want to ensure that the bank remains well capitalised with adequate liquidity levels and that it is able to meet the financial standards laid down by the regulator. Shell banks may not be permitted.

◆ The importance of the bank in its home jurisdiction. The regulator may seek comfort that the bank is of systematic importance in their home jurisdiction, which in turn should be capable of supporting them financially if ever needed. The home jurisdiction should be considered as an equivalent jurisdiction in terms of the AML/CFT measures that it applies.

◆ The competence and experience of the principal persons. The management and staff of the bank must be suitably qualified either by experience or qualifications to be sufficiently competent in the relevant areas of banking and the regulator will assess the risks involved if there are any dominant controllers.

◆ The organisation's systems and controls. The applicant should be committed to complying with any regulatory requirements (e.g. laws and codes of practice) and should have adequate policies and procedures in place to enable it to do so. This will include having good corporate governance systems in place including non-executive directors where necessary.

◆ The ownership and control of the bank. An offshore centre may prefer its banks to be public quoted companies or subsidiaries of one. The ownership structure of the bank must be such that it is clear to the regulator who the ultimate owners and controllers are. This enables the regulator to perform 'fit and proper' checks on these principal persons.

As well as the general licence conditions, the regulator may impose specific licence conditions on certain banks to reflect their particular circumstances.

4.1 Ongoing banking supervision

Licensed banks are usually subject to ongoing supervision by the offshore centre's regulator. The regulator may be known as a financial services commission.

Ongoing supervision by regulators of banking business may include:

◆ on-site examinations conducted at the bank's premises and regular meetings with the bank;

◆ off-site supervision which may include a desk-based analysis of regulatory and statistical returns and other information;

◆ the requirement for the bank to submit annual audited financial statements;

◆ a requirement for the **principal persons** (e.g. directors and shareholders) and key persons (e.g. the money laundering reporting officer and the compliance officer) to be in receipt of an approval by the regulator, or in some cases a no objection letter before they may be appointed to act on behalf of the business;

◆ a requirement to notify the regulator of significant events or changes within the business; and

◆ a requirement to participate in thematic studies where requested to do so by the regulator.

Principal persons
Those individuals who control an organisation by way of directorships or shareholdings.

The regulators in offshore centres will be keen to show that their supervisory approach and performance is compliant with the international standards.

In some jurisdictions, the regulation of banks is undertaken by a separate body to that which regulates other financial services. For example, in the Mauritius, the financial services sector is regulated and supervised by two independent institutions, namely the Bank of Mauritius, for all deposit-taking and foreign exchange matters, and the Financial Services Commission, for non-bank financial services such as insurance.

Codes of practice

Regulators often issue codes of practice using powers that are provided in the regulatory laws. These establish sound principles and requirements that are to be upheld by businesses conducting banking business. Codes of practice may include the following requirements.

◆ The business must be conducted with integrity.

◆ A business must have due regard for the interests of its customers.

◆ A business must organise and control its affairs effectively for the proper performance of its business activities and be able to demonstrate the existence of adequate risk management systems (i.e. uphold customer due diligence and AML and CFT legislation).

◆ A business must be transparent in its business arrangements.

◆ A business must maintain and be able to demonstrate the existence of adequate capital resources including minimum capital requirements, risk asset ration and concentration risk.

◆ A business must deal with the authorities in an open and cooperative manner.

◆ A business must not make statements that are misleading, false or deceptive.

5. Managed banks

Some banks cannot meet the criteria to undertake banking business on their own. These banks may be established as managed banks, meaning that the business of the bank is managed by another registered deposit taker (the manager) within the offshore centre. The manager provides all necessary resources, such as staff, premises and information systems, and operates those resources on behalf of the managed bank. The managed bank is a registered person in its own right, however, and must comply with all aspects of the regulatory framework. The managed bank itself remains ultimately accountable to its regulator for the activities that it undertakes.

The fit and proper assessments in respect of the managed bank are undertaken on the manager. In assessing the fitness and properness of a managed bank, the regulator will apply the same standards as a non-managed bank. A managed bank is sometimes known as an administered bank.

5.1 Advantages of a managed bank

◆ It allows an organisation that may not otherwise meet the criteria for undertaking business in the jurisdiction to operate with the oversight of a manager to ensure that the laws and codes of practice designed to protect the public are maintained.

◆ Costs should be reduced (e.g. the costs of employing staff and renting premises).

◆ It provides administrative efficiencies at the outset by avoiding the need to recruit staff or apply for a licence or permit to employ staff.

◆ The organisation can avoid much of the learning curve that is experienced by a new organisation as its manager provides experienced staff, a procedural framework that should allow it to comply with the laws and codes immediately, premises and information technology.

◆ A managed bank allows a bank to provide offshore services to its existing customer base while taking advantage of the expertise, systems and controls that are already available from the manager.

A managed bank that has established itself within an offshore centre can apply to become a stand-alone bank when it can meet the criteria for licensing set out by the regulator.

Test yourself 8.4

Identify four reasons why a bank may establish itself as a managed bank.

6. Banking secrecy laws

Banking secrecy is a legal principle in some offshore centres under which banks are not allowed to provide authorities with information about their customers.

Switzerland is an example of a jurisdiction where banking secrecy has been a long-standing practice which was formalised in its legislation more recently. Article 47 of the Swiss Federal Act on Banks and Savings Banks provides for imprisonment of up to three years or a fine if a person deliberately discloses a secret that is entrusted to them in their capacity as an employee of the bank.

Banking secrecy legislation would not protect criminals responsible for serious crimes; however, in Switzerland, tax evasion which is now deemed unacceptable in most jurisdictions is not considered to be a crime (although tax fraud is). The Organisation for Economic Cooperation and Development has applied pressure to such offshore centres and they have suffered reputational damage as a result of their banking secrecy legislation (see Chapter 6).

Other bank secrecy jurisdictions include Andorra, Liechtenstein, Austria and Luxembourg.

Chapter summary

◆ Offshore banking is simply having a bank account outside of one's own country of residence.

◆ Advantages of using an offshore bank for the customer include the receipt of gross interest, statutory secrecy or confidentiality provisions that enhance the normal common law principles that apply to the customer/banker relationship and, in some cases, less stringent regulation and supervision that enable cost savings to be passed on to customers by way of higher interest rates.

◆ The main disadvantage of offshore banking is the lack of depositor compensation schemes in some offshore centres.

◆ Banks may wish to offer services from an offshore location in order to benefit from lower taxation, less stringent regulation and supervision, lower costs for premises and staff, and in order to extend the services that it can offer to its existing client base.

◆ When choosing an offshore bank, the quality of the banks within the jurisdiction, the regulator requirements and oversight, the absence of bank failures and the availability of a depositor compensation scheme may all be relevant considerations.

◆ Services provided by offshore banks are similar to those available onshore and include current accounts, deposits and savings accounts, lending facilities, foreign exchange transactions and forward exchange contracts.

◆ The foreign exchange market is a decentralised global marketplace. Banks facilitate currency exchange and can advise customers with known foreign currency invoices to pay what the cost of settling the invoice may be. Banks may also enter into binding forward exchange contracts with customers which obligate the customer to buy or sell a given quantity of a foreign currency at a future date, at a rate of exchange that is determined when the contract is made.

◆ The Group of International Finance Centre Supervisors (formerly known as the Offshore Group of Banking Supervisors) has made it a condition of membership that offshore centres must demonstrate a clear commitment to the implementation of the Core Principles set by the Basel Committee on Banking Supervision (BCBS).

◆ The BCBS is a standard-setting body on all aspects of banking supervision that is best known for its international standards on capital adequacy (the Basel Capital Accord) and its Core Principles for Effective Banking Supervision. These Core Principles are a voluntary framework of minimum standards for sound banking supervisory practices.

◆ The Core Principles state that an effective system of banking supervision needs to be based upon a number of preconditions including sound and sustainable macro-economic policies, a well-developed public infrastructure, effective market discipline and mechanisms for providing an appropriate level of systemic protection.

◆ Banking is usually a regulated activity and banks must therefore obtain a licence from their regulator in order to operate from within their jurisdiction. The regulator usually undertakes a fit and proper assessment of the applicant which may involve assessing its track record, its stature, the competence and experience of its principal persons, its owners and its risk profile.

◆ Once licensed, a bank will be subject to ongoing supervision by its regulator which may include on-site examinations and desk-based analysis of information. In order to facilitate ongoing supervision, the regulator or the jurisdiction's regulations may impose obligations upon licence holders – for example, a requirement for principal persons to be approved by the regulator and for the bank to notify the regulator of significant events or changes within the business.

◆ Regulators may issue codes of practice that establish sound principles to be upheld by businesses conducting banking business. Such codes include key principles such as a requirement to operate with integrity, with adequate capital resources and to deal with the authorities in an open and cooperative manner.

◆ Banks that cannot meet the criteria to undertake banking business on their own may be established as managed banks, meaning that the business of the bank is managed by another registered deposit taker within the offshore centre. When a bank is managed, the manager provides all necessary resources such as staff and premises, and operates those on behalf of the managed bank.

◆ Banking secrecy is a legal principle in some offshore centres under which banks are not allowed to provide authorities with information about their customers. A lot of attention from the international community is attracted to the offshore centres that are known as banking secrecy jurisdictions, not all of which is welcome.

Part Five

Regulation and supervision of the offshore services sector

After studying this part, students will gain an understanding of a typical framework of regulation in an offshore centre including primary and secondary legislation, codes of practice and guidance notes. Students will be able to discuss the fit and proper considerations that a regulator may undertake before granting a licence to conduct financial services business and gain an understanding of the ongoing regulation of such entities and the process that the Financial Services Authority (FSA) uses in order to decide upon the level of ongoing supervision that it applies to regulated organisations. Students will be able to explain the objectives, powers and general functions of the financial services regulator in the UK, the FSA, and will be able to discuss its principles-based approach to regulation. Other important legislation that is addressed in this part includes the Data Protection Act 1998, the criminal insider dealing legislation and the behaviours that constitute the civil offence of 'market abuse'. Students will gain an understanding of the main aims of the Retail Distribution Review and its impact on offshore centres, and will be able to discuss some of the international bodies and standards that have an impact on offshore regulation. In addition, students will gain an understanding of money laundering and why it is considered harmful, and will appreciate the impact that international bodies and AML initiatives have had on the offshore environment. Students will be able to explain a typical AML framework in an offshore jurisdiction and will be able to discuss the various money laundering offences and obligations that the AML legislation imposes on offshore professionals. Students will be able to discuss customer due diligence. Finally, students will gain an understanding of how to recognise money laundering.

Learning outcomes

At the end of this part, students will be able to:

◆ discuss the need for and development of regulation;

◆ explain the regulation of offshore financial services such as trust company business and investment business;

◆ outline what factors a regulator may consider when assessing the fit and proper status of an applicant for a financial services business licence;

◆ explain the typical content of primary and secondary legislation, codes of practice and guidance notes;

◆ explain the objectives, powers and general functions of the FSA;

◆ discuss the FSA's principles of good regulation, principles-based regulation and the FSA's principles for business;

◆ discuss the FSA's ARROW II framework;

◆ discuss the Data Protection Act 1998 and the main principles under the Act;

◆ explain the offence of 'insider dealing', the penalties involved and how insider dealing may be prevented;

◆ explain the behaviours that constitute 'market abuse', the penalties involved and how it may be prevented;

◆ outline the main aims of the FSA's Retail Distribution Review and the impact on offshore centres;

◆ discuss international bodies and standards that have an impact on offshore regulation including IOSCO, the IAIS and the OGIS;

◆ explain what is meant by the term 'money laundering';

◆ explain the traditional model of money laundering;

◆ explain why money laundering is considered harmful;

◆ discuss international bodies and AML initiatives including those of the Basel Committee, the UNODC, the FATF, the EC Council and the Wolfsberg Principles;

◆ explain the principal features of AML frameworks including primary and secondary legislation, and guidance notes such as those of the JMLSG;

◆ explain the substantive offences of money laundering, the offences of 'failure to report' and 'tipping off';

◆ explain the obligations on service providers and individuals in relation to the reporting of suspicious activities;

◆ explain what is meant by 'the subjective test';

◆ discuss CFT legislation and initiatives;

◆ explain the meaning of 'know your customer' and how this differs from 'customer due diligence';

◆ discuss money laundering in offshore centres;

◆ discuss the impact of AML/CFT processes on offshore business;

◆ outline the requirements of a suspicious activity report; and

◆ understand how to recognise money laundering.

Chapter nine

Regulation and supervision of the offshore services sector

List of topics

1. The need for regulation
2. The development of regulation
3. Regulation of offshore financial services
4. Regulation in the UK
5. Data protection
6. Insider dealing
7. Market abuse
8. Retail Distribution Review
9. International bodies

Introduction

This chapter outlines the need for and the development of regulation. The chapter explains what a typical regulatory framework in an offshore centre may consist of and then outlines in more details the regulatory framework in the UK, including the role and powers of the regulator of financial services, the Financial Services Authority (FSA). The important principles of the Data Protection Act 1998 are outlined, as are the offences and associated penalties for non-compliance. The chapter also outlines the insider dealing offences under the Criminal Justice Act 1993 and the behaviours that constitute market abuse under the Financial Services and Markets Act 2000. The chapter outlines the main elements of the Retail Distribution Review, which will raise the standards that investors can expect from investment advisers, and concludes with an outline of the more influential international bodies that have had an influence on regulation of the offshore financial services industry (excluding those that set the AML/CFT standards, as those are discussed in Chapter 10).

1. The need for regulation

The regulation of organisations involved in financial services and investment comprises sets of rules, prohibitions, restrictions and guidelines which are applicable to those financial and investment organisations.

Regulation is necessary in order to maintain financial markets (both national and international) that are efficient, orderly and fair. Regulation protects consumers from abusive practices and financial crime, thus maintaining the integrity of the financial markets. It is important that only experienced professionals who are fit and proper can become involved in providing financial services business. Regulation prohibits anyone who has not been approved by the regulator from providing financial services and sets out what these organisations can and cannot do. It provides for those who do not meet the desired standard to be sanctioned or prevented from operating where appropriate.

2. The development of regulation

In May 1997, the supervision of banking and investment services was merged into the Securities and Investments board (SIB). The SIB formally changed its name to the Financial Services Authority (FSA) in October 1997.

Responsibility for banking supervision was transferred to the FSA from the Bank of England. In May 2000, the FSA took over the role of the UK Listing Authority (UKLA) from the London Stock Exchange.

The Financial Services and Markets Act (FSMA) transferred to the FSA responsibility for several other organisations including the Investment Management Regulatory Authority, the Personal Investment Authority and the Securities and Futures Authority. In 2005, the FSA took responsibility for the regulation of general insurance business in order to implement the EU Insurance Mediation directive.

2.1 The future of regulation in the UK

In June 2010, the Chancellor announced the government's intention to restructure the UK's financial regulatory framework. As part of this regulatory reform, the FSA will be replaced with two new successor regulatory bodies.

In 2013, the FSA will be replaced by two new regulatory bodies, the Prudential Regulation Authority (the PRA) which will be a subsidiary of the Bank of England and responsible for regulating deposit taking businesses, insurers and investment banks and the Financial Conduct Authority (the FCA) which will be responsible for the regulation of conduct in retail and wholesale financial markets, and the infrastructure that supports those markets.

The FSA is now in the process of making changes to its structure in order to prepare for the restructure.

3. Regulation of offshore financial services

Regulatory frameworks in the UK (and many other onshore jurisdictions) have been heavily influenced by international bodies and initiatives. While many offshore centres are not compelled to incorporate international initiatives into their own regulatory frameworks, many have chosen to do so as they recognise that it is important to embrace the efforts of the international community and conduct their business with equivalent standards. This is essential in order to maintain investors' confidence, to attract foreign investment and to develop or maintain a reputation that allows offshore centres to compete without sanction.

3.1 Primary legislation

Regulatory frameworks for financial services industries offshore typically comprise primary legislation, secondary legislation, regulatory codes and guidance notes.

The primary legislation is usually equivalent to the UK's Financial Services and Markets Act 2000 (FSMA). It is usual for the primary legislation to provide for the creation of a regulator (equivalent to the FSA) which in offshore centres is often referred to as a financial services commission. The primary legislation usually provides for a general prohibition against the provision of financial services without authorisation. The regulator is granted powers to authorise organisations to provide financial services business, supervise that the jurisdictions laws, orders and codes are adhered to, and provide for enforcement and sanctioning powers when they are not. Sanctions may include the regulator imposing fines, banning individuals from working within the finance industry or making a public statement about their conduct.

Stop and think 9.1

What sanctions has the regulator in your jurisdiction imposed recently?

Authorisation is usually only granted to 'fit and proper' applicants.

The fit and proper test
The fit and proper test may be set in the law (as they are in the FSMA) or may be influenced by a policy that is set by the regulator. A fit and proper determination by the regulator may include factors such as the following.

◆ **A relevant and satisfactory track record:** The regulator will prefer organisations that have a demonstrable track record. Where an organisation has a track record in another jurisdiction, the regulator may ask the regulator in that jurisdiction whether they hold any adverse information in connection with it. Where the organisation is a new company that cannot demonstrate a track record, the regulator can look instead to that of its proposed controllers (directors and shareholders).

◆ **The integrity of the applicant:** An assessment of the integ
the organisation will to some extent reflect the integrity of i'
management team and the individuals employed by it. In a'
integrity of the organisation or its management, the regula
its past conduct.

◆ **Competence of the staff employed:** An assessment of
qualified and experienced staff employed by the organis
regulator in determining its overall competency.

◆ **The financial standing of the applicant:** The financ
available to the applicant and how financial risks will b
to the entity remaining as a going concern. The regulator may requ...
applicant to have adequate professional indemnity insurance.

◆ **The resources available to the organisation:** The jurisdiction may
require the organisation to have local management and control (i.e. a
majority of the directors being located within the jurisdiction) of the
organisation and local premises.

◆ **The structure of the organisation:** An assessment of the structure/
organisation of the applicant may include an assessment of the availability
of resources to the organisation, the systems and controls, and the
transparency of ownership.

The structure of the organisation will need to provide for sufficient oversight
by its senior management. The systems and controls of the organisation must
be sufficient to manage risk and the affairs of the organisation effectively.
Good corporate governance is key to demonstrate a well-run and effective
organisation.

Transparency of ownership is very important to an offshore regulator. It is
important that it can identify the ultimate controllers. A company that is owned
by a structure involving trusts and companies can be a severe hindrance to the
transparency of a structure and, for this reason, it is unlikely that the regulator
would permit a structure without imposing additional safeguards (such as
written undertakings or the involvement of regulated trustees) to ensure that it
can always identify and perform due diligence on those who are in control.

3.2 Secondary legislation

Secondary legislation (sometimes referred to as regulations, orders or
ordinances) uses powers granted to it in the primary legislation; it supplements
the primary legislation and places additional more detailed requirements on
authorised persons.

3.3 Codes of practice

The regulators are usually authorised to publish regulatory codes, referred to as
codes of practice which usually contain provisions that are similar to the FSA's
principles for business (see section 4.7 below).

Failure to follow the codes of practice shall not of itself render any person liable to proceedings of any kind or invalidate any transaction, but the codes may be used as evidence in any proceedings if it appears to the court to be relevant to any questions arising in the proceedings, and shall be taken into account in determining any such questions.

3.4 Guidance

Guidance may outline the requirements of the jurisdiction's primary and secondary legislation (the statutory requirements) on a particular subject matter and present ways in which authorised organisations may comply with the statutory requirements. Guidance assists service providers through practical interpretation of the requirements of the regulator. Guidance may emphasise or promote a particular approach desired by the regulator and assists authorised organisations to develop their systems and controls accordingly.

The content of the guidance is considered to be a regulatory requirement and failure to follow it may result in a regulatory sanction. Guidance may be taken into account when deciding whether or not a person has committed an offence under the law.

In a well-regulated jurisdiction, a failure to follow the guidance is considered to be a serious matter and, as well as legal action, it may form the basis for regulatory action by the regulator.

3.5 Regulation of trust and company service providers

In the offshore environment, trust company business service providers may typically be regulated in accordance with section 3 of this chapter. In the UK, the provision of trust and company service providers is not as prevalent as it is offshore. The approach to the regulation of organisations that provide such services differs somewhat from that of the offshore centres. In the UK, trust and company service providers do not fall within the scope of the FSMA. Instead, there is a requirement under the Money Laundering Regulations 2007 for such service providers to register with HM Revenue & Customs (HMRC) for AML purposes. The definition of what constitutes trust and company service providers is largely in line with those of the offshore centres, as detailed in section 2 of Chapter 4. HMRC is the main supervisory authority for trust and company service providers.

In order to gain a further understanding of the regulatory frameworks surrounding financial services business, the UK's framework will be discussed in some detail.

Test yourself 9.1

Outline a typical regulatory framework in an offshore centre.

4. Regulation in the UK

4.1 The Financial Services Authority

The Financial Services Authority (FSA) is an independent, non-governmental body which has been given statutory powers and objectives by the Financial Services and Markets Act 2000 (FSMA), which came into force on 1 December 2001 and is the primary legislation in the UK.

The board of the FSA is appointed by and accountable to HM Treasury and has responsibility for the FSA's overall policy. Day-to-day decisions are the responsibility of the executive committee.

4.2 The FSA's regulatory objectives

The FSMA gives the FSA the following four regulatory objectives.

Table 10.1: The FSA's regulatory objectives.

Objective	Description
1. Market confidence	To maintain confidence in the financial system (i.e. financial markets and exchanges, regulated activities and other connected activities).
2. Financial stability	To contribute to the protection and enhancement of the stability of the UK financial system.
3. The protection of consumers	To secure the appropriate degree of protection for consumers.
4. The reduction of financial crime	To reduce the extent to which it is possible for a business carried on by a regulated person (or a person acting without the necessary authorisation to act) to be used for a purpose connected with financial crime.

4.3 Powers of the FSA

The FSMA gives the FSA a wide range of powers that it may use in order to achieve its objectives. The FSA has the power to grant an authorisation to conduct a regulated activity, to vary any authorisation granted and also to withdraw such an authorisation. The FSA has rule-making powers and has powers to investigate and gather information in order to assess whether an authorised person is abiding by any such rules or regulations. The FSA has enforcement powers and can appoint a person to hold an inquiry, can issue prohibition orders, holds disciplinary powers and can impose penalties – for example, in cases of market abuse.

4.4 General functions of the FSA

The FSMA describes the general functions of the FSA as:

◆ making rules under the FSMA;

◆ preparing and issuing codes under the FSMA;

◆ the giving of general guidance; and

◆ determining the general policy and principles by reference to which it performs its functions.

4.5 The FSA's principles of good regulation

Article 2 (3) of the FSMA provides that in discharging the general functions described in section 4.4 of this chapter, the FSA must have regard to the following matters which the FSA refers to as 'principles of good regulation'.

Table 10.2: The FSA's principles of good regulation.

Principle	Description
Efficiency and economy	The FSA should use its resources in the most efficient and economic way. The non-executive committee of the FSA is required to oversee its allocation of resources and to report to HM Treasury each year.
The role of management	The FSA holds a firm's senior management responsible for ensuring that it complies with the regulatory requirements. Authorised firms must therefore take reasonable care to clarify each individual's responsibilities to ensure that the affairs of the firm can be adequately monitored and controlled.
Proportionality	The restrictions that the FSA imposes on the financial services industry must be proportionate to the benefits that are expected to result from those restrictions. In making judgements, the FSA takes into account the costs to firms and consumers. The FSA uses a cost-benefit analysis in relation to its proposed regulatory requirements.
Innovation	The FSA facilitates innovation in connection with regulated activities so far as possible. The FSA may therefore allow for different methods of compliance so as not to restrict market participants unduly from launching new financial products and services.
International character	The international character of financial services and markets and the desirability of maintaining the competitive position of the UK. This involves dealing with overseas regulatory bodies in a cooperative manner in order to agree international standards and to monitor global firms and markets.

Principle	Description
Competition	The need to minimise the adverse effects on competition that may arise from anything that is done by the FSA in the discharging of its functions and also to facilitate competition between those who are subject to any form of regulation by the FSA. These principles are aimed at avoiding unnecessary regulatory barriers to entry or business expansion.

4.6 Principles-based regulation

Over the last few years, the FSA has moved more towards principles-based regulation which complements the risk-based regulation. Principles-based regulation means (where possible) moving away from dictating through detailed prescriptive rules and allowing businesses to decide how they can best meet the regulatory requirements with emphasis on principles and desirable outcomes. The FSA's high-level 'principles for business' are discussed in section 4.7 of this chapter.

The motivation for the focus on principles-based regulation was in part to relieve the burden on the financial services industry of having to keep up with the large volumes of ever-expanding rules, to allow regulation to respond quickly to changes in the financial services industry and because such prescriptive rules have not been able to prevent misconduct and other undesirable outcomes.

4.7 The FSA's principles for business

The FSA's 11 principles for business are contained in the FSA Handbook and are fundamental obligations of all firms under the regulatory system. The principles are as follows.

Table 10.3: The FSA's principles for business.

Principle	Description
1. Integrity	A firm must conduct its business with integrity.
2. Skill, care and diligence	A firm must conduct its business with due skill, care and diligence.
3. Management and control	A firm must take reasonable care to organise and control its affairs responsibly and effectively, with adequate risk management systems.
4. Financial prudence	A firm must maintain adequate financial resources.
5. Market conduct	A firm must observe proper standards of market conduct.

Principle	Description
6. Customers' interests	A firm must pay due regard to the interests of its customers and treat them fairly.
7. Communications with clients	A firm must pay due regard to the information needs of its clients and communicate information to them in a way which is clear, fair and not misleading.
8. Conflicts of interest	A firm must manage conflicts of interest fairly, both between itself and its customers, and between a customer and another client.
9. Customers: relationships of trust	A firm must take reasonable care to ensure the suitability of its advice and discretionary decisions for any customer who is entitled to rely upon its judgement.
10. Clients' assets	A firm must arrange adequate protection for clients' assets when it is responsible for them.
11. Relations with regulators	A firm must deal with its regulators in an open and cooperative way, and must disclose to the FSA appropriately anything to the firm of which the FSA would reasonably expect notice.

Test yourself 9.2

State four of the FSA's principles for business.

4.8 The FSA Handbook

The FSA publishes a single Handbook of rules and guidance (the FSA Handbook) for all authorised firms carrying out financial services business in the UK.

4.9 Authorisation to conduct regulated activity

The FSMA contains a general prohibition on carrying out a regulated activity in the UK unless the person doing so is a person authorised under the FSMA to do so or is an exempt person.

When an application is made to the FSA for permission to carry on a regulated activity, the FSA must ensure that the applicant will satisfy (and continue to satisfy) certain threshold conditions which are set out in schedule 6 to the FSMA.

The threshold conditions vary depending on the regulatory activity to which the application relates; however, in general, the conditions that must be met in order for the FSA to authorise a person under the FSMA relate to:

◆ the legal status of the applicant (in some instances the applicant must be a company);

- the location of the offices of the applicant (which should be in the UK);
- any close links with persons that are likely to prevent effective supervision by the FSA;
- the resources of the applicant (resources must be adequate); and
- the suitability of the applicant (the applicant must be a fit and proper person).

4.10 Ongoing supervision by the FSA

Persons who are authorised to conduct a regulated activity by the FSA are subject to ongoing supervision by the FSA.

The FSA uses a framework to assess the risk that an authorised person poses to its regulatory objectives (described in section 4.2 of this chapter). The current framework (introduced in August 2006) is known as ARROW II (the advanced risk responsive operating framework).

The ARROW II process identifies risks to the FSA's statutory objectives and allows it to measure and mitigate the risk, and provides for risk monitoring and reporting. The FSA combines the probability of the risk materialising and the impact of the problem event if it were to occur, to give it a measure of the overall risk posed to its statutory objectives. This measure is then used to classify a firm as presenting either a low, a medium low, a medium high or a high risk. The FSA's assessment of the risks posed by a firm will determine the overall intensity of its regulatory approach to supervising it and the level of resource allocated to doing so.

Within ARROW II, the FSA may use one of two basic approaches (or a mixture of the two) that the FSA uses to supervise firms: the ARROW firms approach, which is used when assessing risks in individual firms (referred to by the FSA as vertical supervision), and the ARROW themes approach, which is used when assessing risks that may involve several firms or relate to the market as a whole. The FSA refers to this as 'horizontal work'.

Test yourself 9.3

What is the FSA's ARROW II process designed to achieve?

5. Data protection

5.1 The Data Protection Act 1998

The Data Protection Act 1998 (DPA) was designed to implement the EU Data Protection Directive which requires member states to protect the privacy rights and freedoms of individuals in the processing of personal data.

The DPA refers to organisations that process data as **data controllers**. The DPA is applicable whenever a data controller processes personal and/

Data controller
An organisation that processes personal data.

or sensitive personal data. The 'processing' of data includes the processing (a wide definition which could include obtaining, storing, retrieving, etc.) of personal data by a computer or recording it in a structured manual filing system. **Personal data** refers to data that relates to a living individual (the data subject) who can be identified from that data. For a system to fall within the scope of the DPA, it must be 'structured' by reference to individuals for it to fall within the scope of the DPA.

Personal data
Data that relates to a living individual (the data subject) who can be identified from that data.

Under the DPA, organisations which process data are required to notify the relevant authority (the Information Commissioner) of the purpose of processing the data and the manner in which they process it. This information is then recorded in a register which may be inspected by the public.

Sensitive personal data under the DPA is personal data that relates to the racial or ethnic origin of the data subject, their political opinions or religious beliefs, whether they are a member of a trade union, their physical or mental health or condition, their sexual life, the commission or alleged commission by them of any offence, or any proceedings for any offence committed or alleged to have been committed by them, the disposal of such proceedings or the sentence of any court in such proceedings.

Data controllers who wish to process sensitive personal data must also satisfy at least one of the conditions detailed within the DPA – for example, the data controller has the explicit consent of the individual or the data controller is required by law to process the data (e.g. for employment purposes), or the processing takes place in order to protect the vital interests of the data subject.

Many offshore centres have legislation that is similar to the DPA and it is highly relevant legislation to offshore service providers which are likely to be considered as data controllers in their own jurisdiction.

Guernsey and Jersey are currently considering the creation of a single data protection commissioner who will be responsible for both Jersey and Guernsey. This is an example of the Crown Dependencies working together to provide a more consistent approach for those who have dealings with the islands and for the benefit of organisations that operate in both islands. The DPA requirements often overlap with (and in some cases conflict with) other legislation that is in force.

Making it work 9.1: Data protection law in Jersey

Jersey's data protection legislation is contained within the Data Protection (Jersey) Law 2005. In 2005, the regulator in Jersey, together with the Data Protection Commissioner, the Law Officer's Department and the Joint Financial Crimes Unit (the island's Financial Intelligence Unit), published guidance for financial services business in response concerns raised by banks and other financial services businesses about the interaction between Jersey's AML legislation and its data protection legislation.

The concerns surrounded the obligation not to 'tip off' an individual about whom a suspicious activity report (SAR) has been made on the one hand, and an individual's right of access to their personal data under the 'subject access' provisions of the data protection legislation on the other.

While there are exemptions from the subject access provisions, in any case, to the extent to which the disclosure of that personal data in response to a subject access request would lead to the commission of a **tipping off** offence under AML legislation, the guidance concluded that it should never be assumed that the exemptions apply automatically to SARs and that each time a subject access request is received, the business concerned must carefully consider whether, in that particular case, disclosure of the information in the SAR would be likely to prejudice the prevention or detection of crime, or the regulation of financial services, or lead to an offence of tipping off.

Tipping off
This refers to the committing of an offence under Article 333 of the PoCA.

5.2 Principles of the Data Protection Act

In order to comply with the DPA, a data controller must adhere to eight principles which are as follows.

1. Personal data shall be processed fairly and lawfully.
2. Personal data shall be obtained only for one or more specified and lawful purposes.
3. Personal data shall be adequate, relevant and not excessive in relation to the purpose or purposes for which they are processed.
4. Personal data shall be accurate and kept up to date (where necessary).
5. Personal data processed shall not be kept for longer than is necessary for the purpose for which it was processed.
6. Personal data shall be processed in accordance with the rights of data subjects under the Act.
7. Appropriate measures shall be taken against unauthorised or unlawful processing of personal data.
8. Personal data shall not be transferred to a country or territory outside of the European Economic Area unless that country or territory ensures an adequate level of protection for the rights and freedoms of data subjects.

5.3 Offences under the DPA

The following are offences under the DPA.

- Processing personal data without notification.
- Failure to notify the Information Commissioner of changes to those notified.
- Making a false statement in response to an information notice.
- Obstructing a warrant holder.
- Unlawfully obtaining and/or selling of personal data.

5.4 Penalties for non-compliance with the DPA

If the information Commissioner believes that a data controller has not complied with any of the DPA principles, they can issue an enforcement notice to stop processing or comply with the principles.

Offences under the DPA are criminal; however, they do not carry prison sentences. Offences under the DPA can be prosecuted by the Office of the Information Commissioner and can be tried in either a magistrate's court or a crown court, depending on the seriousness of the case. If brought in a magistrate's court, the maximum fine is £5,000, and if tried in the crown court, upon conviction, an unlimited fine can be imposed.

Test yourself 9.4

State four offences under the Data Protection Act 1998.

6. Insider dealing

Insider dealing is a criminal offence under the Criminal Justice Act 1993 which came into force on 1 March 1994.

Insider dealing
Insider dealing occurs when an individual with inside information (price-sensitive information) uses this information in relation to securities (that are price-affected) in order to make a profit (or avoid a loss), thus gaining an advantage that would not be available to the general public.

Insider dealing occurs when an individual with inside information (price-sensitive information) uses this information in relation to securities (that are price-affected) in order to make a profit (or avoid a loss), thus gaining an advantage that would not be available to the general public.

The price-affected securities stated in schedule 2 of the Act include:

◆   shares and share capital of companies;
◆   debt securities including debentures, debenture stock, loan stock and certificates of deposits;
◆   warrants;
◆   depository receipts;
◆   options;
◆   futures; and
◆   contracts for differences.

6.1 Insider dealing offences

There are three offences which constitute insider dealing. These are:

1.   dealing in securities on the basis of inside information;
2.   encouraging another to deal on the basis of inside information; and
3.   disclosing inside information otherwise than in the proper performance of the functions of employment or profession.

For an offence to have been committed, the acquisition or disposal must have occurred on a regulated market, or if the person relies on or is acting as a professional intermediary.

For the purposes of insider dealing, **inside information** is information which relates to particular securities, is specific or precise, has not been made public and if it were made public, would be likely to have a significant effect on the price of any securities.

No offence is committed if the insider did not know that the information was 'inside information'. The information must have been obtained by virtue of being a director, employee or shareholder of an issuer of securities (or the direct or indirect source of the information is one of these people), or by having access to the information by virtue of their employment, office or profession.

Inside information
Information which relates to particular securities, is specific or precise, has not been made public and if it were made public, would be likely to have a significant effect on the price of any securities.

6.2 Insider dealing defences

Under Article 53, an individual will not be guilty of insider dealing if, in relation to the dealing offence or the encouraging another person to deal offence, they can show that they:

◆ did not expect that a profit attributable to the inside information would be made;

◆ believed (on reasonable grounds) that the information had been disclosed widely enough that none of those taking part in the dealing would be prejudiced by not having the information; and

◆ would have dealt in the securities anyway.

In relation to the 'disclosure of information' offence, it is a defence to show that they did not expect:

◆ any person to deal in the securities as a result of the disclosure; or

◆ the dealing to make a profit attributable to the inside information.

6.3 Penalties

The maximum penalty for an individual convicted of insider dealing is a fine or imprisonment for a term not exceeding seven years, or both.

Making it work 9.2: Prosecuting insider dealing

In March 2009, the FSA secured its first insider dealing conviction against a solicitor, Mr Christopher McQuoid, and his father-in-law, Mr Melbourne.

In the FSA's first insider dealing prosecution to reach trial, the jury found that Mr McQuoid, who had acted as the legal counsel to TTP Communications (TTP) had passed inside information about a planned takeover of TTP by Motorola to Mr Melbourne who profited as a result of a trade that was made based on the information.

Two days before the takeover of TTP was made public, Mr Melbourne brought 153,824 TTP shares at 13 pence per share. When the takeover was announced at an agreed share price of 45 pence per share, Mr Melbourne made a profit of £48,919.20 which he later split with Mr McQuoid.

Both were found guilty and were sentenced to eight months' imprisonment (although Mr Melbourne's was suspended).

As at 4 August 2011, the FSA has secured 10 convictions relating to insider dealing.

7. Market abuse

Market abuse
Behaviour in relation to investments which are trading (or have applied to trade) on a UK market.

Part VIII of the FSMA sets out the behaviour which amounts to **market abuse**. This involves behaviour in relation to investments which are trading (or have applied to trade) on a UK market. Seven types of behaviour can amount to market abuse.

Table 10.4: Types of market abuse.

Type of market abuse	Description
1. Insider dealing	Where an insider deals or attempts to deal in a qualifying investment on the basis of inside information relating to the investment.
2. Improper disclosure of inside information	Where an insider discloses information to another person otherwise than in the proper course of exercise of their employment, profession or duties.
3. Misuse of information	This is behaviour that is based on information that is not generally available to those using the market but would, if available to a regular user, be relevant to their decisions about the terms on which to deal.
4. Manipulating transactions	This behaviour includes effecting transactions or orders to trade which may give a false or misleading impression as to the supply of or demand for an investment or to secure the price of an investment at an abnormal or artificial level.
5. Manipulating devices	This involves effecting transactions or orders to trade which employ fictitious devices or any form of deception or contrivance. This could involve spreading misleading information with a view to increasing the price of a shareholding and thereby giving others a false impression of the share price.

Type of market abuse	Description
6. Dissemination	The dissemination of information that gives a false or misleading impression about an investment by a person who knew (or could reasonably have been expected to have known) that the information was false or misleading.
7. Distortion and misleading behaviour	This is behaviour which is likely to give a regular user of the market a false or misleading impression as to the supply of or demand for an investment or that otherwise distorts the market in an investment.

For the purposes of the market abuse offences, an 'insider' is a person who has inside information. Inside information is information of a precise nature which is not generally available and that would, if generally available, be likely to have a significant effect on the price of the investment. The FSMA describes information as being precise if it indicates circumstances that exist or may reasonably be expected to come into existence, or an event that has or is expected to occur, and is specific enough to enable a conclusion to be drawn as to the possible effect on the price of the investment.

Market abuse is not a criminal offence and so conviction will not result in a jail sentence. Civil penalties may be imposed, however, and these could include unlimited fines.

As market abuse is a civil rather than a criminal offence, the FSA needs only to prove that the behaviour was illegal on the balance of probabilities. This should mean that it may be able to secure a conviction for insider dealing under the market abuse provisions of the FSMA where it may not be able to secure one under the Criminal Justice Act 1993.

Test yourself 9.5

Distinguish between the offence of insider dealing under the Criminal Justice Act 1993 and the offence of market abuse under the FSMA.

8. Retail Distribution Review

In June 2006, the FSA announced the Retail Distribution Review (RDR), which had the specific aim of identifying and addressing the causes of problems in relation to the retail investment market. The RDR is intended to raise the standards investors can expect from all investment advisers and should bring the following benefits.

◆ Consumers will better understand the advice service they are being offered.

◆ Independent advice will be truly independent and relate to a wider range of products.

◆ Adviser recommendations will not be influenced by the commission paid by product providers.

◆ Consumers will know upfront how much advice is costing them and how they will pay for it.

◆ Advisers will be better qualified and will keep their knowledge up to date.

There are three main elements to the RDR, which are as follows.

1. **Adviser charging:** This element aims to ensure that consumers are offered a transparent and fair charging system for the advice they receive.

2. **Independent advice:** This element aims to ensure that consumers are clear about the services that they receive.

3. **Professionalism:** This element aims to ensure that consumers receive advice from highly respected professionals, thereby inspiring confidence and building trust.

In order to implement the above-mentioned elements, the FSA has published new rules that will come into effect on 31 December 2012 and will apply to all advisers in the retail investment market, regardless of the type of firm they work for (banks, product providers, independent financial advisers, wealth managers or stockbrokers).

In relation to the 'adviser charging' element, the new rules set out that advisers will set their own charges and separately charge clients for their services as they will no longer be able to receive commission set by product providers (product providers will be banned from offering commission to advisers). Charging structures will need to be based on the level of service that they provide in future rather than on a particular provider or product that they recommend. Advisers will need to be upfront with consumers in disclosing their charges and ongoing charges should only be levied where an ongoing service has been agreed with the client.

In relation to the 'independent advice' element, the new rules will require advisers to describe their services clearly as either independent or restricted. If they declare themselves to be independent, they need to consider a broader range of products beyond packaged products. Independent advisers will need to be able to provide unbiased, unrestricted advice based on a comprehensive and fair analysis of the relevant market.

In relation to the 'professionalism' element, the new rules will require that advisers hold a statement of professional standing issued by a body accredited by the FSA, hold an appropriate qualification (and complete a 'gap fill' which brings the qualification up to the desired standard where required) and observe a code of ethics that advisers are subject to as an approved person.

8.1 The impact of the RDR on offshore centres

Although the RDR is only applicable in the UK, the regulators in many offshore centres have made public statements informing organisations that conduct investment business about the action that they will take to bring the legislation in their jurisdiction in line with the new standards imposed by the RDR. The Isle of Man, for example, wrote to all chief executives of organisations licensed to conduct investment business and set out that it is 'committed to maintaining its reputation as a well regulated financial centre and sees that implementing an RDR type regime is key to this'.

It will take some time before RDR measures are implemented in offshore centres and there will no doubt be some differences between the UK's RDR and the measures that offshore centres will put in place. However, the aim of the offshore centres will be similar to those of the RDR.

Test yourself 9.6

What are the three main elements of the RDR?

9. International bodies

The standards set by international bodies such as the International Organization of Securities Commissions (IOSCO) and the International Association of Insurance Supervisors have had an impact on the regulation of financial services business. Other bodies such as the Offshore Group of Insurance Supervisors also play a useful role to offshore financial services business providers.

9.1 The International Organization of Securities Commissions

The roots of the IOSCO were first established in 1974 when it was only an inter-American regional association. However, its then 11 members (securities agencies from North and South America) decided at its 1983 annual conference in Quito, Ecuador to develop into a global cooperative body.

In 1984, securities regulators from France, Indonesia, South Korea and the UK were the first to join the IOSCO from outside the Americas. The IOSCO claims that its membership regulates over 95% of the world's securities markets. It is the primary forum for securities market regulatory agencies with its members being drawn from over 100 jurisdictions. The FSA is the UK's member.

The role of the IOSCO

The IOSCO is recognised as the international standard-setter for securities markets and it provides comprehensive technical assistance to its members including those regulating emerging markets.

IOSCO objectives

The objectives and principles of securities regulation were last revisited in June 2010 and consist of 38 principles of securities regulation which are based upon the following three objectives:

1. protecting investors;

2. ensuring that markets are fair, efficient and transparent; and

3. reducing systemic risk.

The principles must be implemented practically under the relevant legal framework in order to achieve the above-mentioned objectives.

IOSCO Principles

In 1998, the IOSCO adopted a comprehensive set of Objectives and Principles of Securities Regulation, referred to as the IOSCO Principles. These are now recognised as the international benchmark for all securities markets.

The IOSCO Principles are grouped into the following nine categories:

1. principles relating to the regulator;

2. principles for self-regulation;

3. principles for the enforcement of securities regulation;

4. principles for cooperation in regulation;

5. principles for issuers;

6. principles for auditor, credit rating agencies and other information service providers;

7. principles for collective investment schemes;

8. principles for market intermediaries; and

9. principles for secondary markets.

In 2003, the organisation endorsed a comprehensive methodology that was designed to enable an objective assessment of the level of implementation of the IOSCO Principles by member jurisdictions.

The Multilateral Memorandum of Understanding

The Multilateral Memorandum of Understanding (MMOU) was developed following the terrorist attacks on the USA on 11 September 2001. It is designed to facilitate cross-border enforcement and exchange of information between international securities regulators. The regulators of offshore centres such as Guernsey, Jersey, the Isle of Man, Bermuda and the British Virgin Islands are all signatories to the MMOU Concerning Consultation and Cooperation and the Exchange of Information.

The IOSCO endorsed the MMOU as the benchmark for international cooperation among securities regulators.

In 2005, the IOSCO decided that all members with primary responsibility for securities regulation in their jurisdiction should have applied for (and been accepted as) signatories under the MMOU or expressed a commitment to seek legal authority to enable them to become signatories before the target date.

The MMOU sets out how signatories will cooperate and exchange information for securities regulation purposes such as the investigation of insider dealing and market manipulation activities.

Test yourself 9.7

What are the IOSCO Principles?

9.2 The International Association of Insurance Supervisors

The International Association of Insurance Supervisors (IAIS) was established in 1994 and represents insurance regulators and supervisors of approximately 190 jurisdictions. Since 1999 it has permitted insurance professionals as observers. Many offshore centres including Jersey, the Isle of Man, the Mauritius and Gibraltar are members of the IAIS.

The IAIS issues global insurance principles, standards and guidance papers. It sets out principles that it deems fundamental to effective insurance supervision.

The Insurance Core Principles serve as a basic benchmark for insurance supervisors in all jurisdictions and are set out under the following six headings:

1.   conditions for effective insurance supervision;
2.   the supervisory system (includes supervisory objectives, authority, process and cooperation and information sharing);
3.   the supervised entity (includes licensing, suitability of persons, changes in control and portfolio transfers, corporate governance and internal control);
4.   ongoing supervision (includes market analysis, reporting to supervisors and off-site monitoring, on-site inspections, preventative and corrective measures, enforcement and or sanctions, winding up and exit from the market and group-wide supervision);
5.   prudential requirements (includes risk assessment and management insurance activity, liabilities, investments, derivatives and similar commitments and capital adequacy and solvency); and
6.   markets and consumers (covers intermediaries and consumer protection).

9.3 The Offshore Group of Insurance Supervisors

The Offshore Group of Insurance Supervisors (OGIS) was founded in 1993 and consists of insurance business regulators and supervisors from offshore jurisdictions. The group has strict criteria which must be met by its members. Jersey, Guernsey, the Isle of Man, the Bahamas, the British Virgin Islands and the Cayman Islands are all members of the OGIS.

The formal objectives of the OGIS are to:

◆ provide mechanisms and forums whereby insurance supervisors from jurisdictions concerned with offshore insurance business may discuss areas of mutual interest and concern, and formulate appropriate policies;

◆ provide assistance and encouragement to appropriate non-member jurisdictions to establish regimes for the supervision of offshore insurance business at least to standards equivalent to those of the group;

◆ represent the interests of the group at international forums; and

◆ promote the proper supervision of offshore insurance business.

Chapter summary

◆ Regulation is necessary in order to maintain financial markets that are efficient, orderly and fair. Regulation protects consumers from abusive practices and financial crime, thus maintaining the integrity of the financial markets.

◆ Regulatory frameworks for financial services industries offshore can be similar to those found onshore and typically comprise primary legislation, secondary legislation, regulatory codes and guidance notes. Many offshore centres incorporate international initiatives into their own regulatory frameworks and conduct their business with equivalent standards.

◆ The Financial Services Authority (FSA) is the regulator of financial services in the UK and the Financial Services and Markets Act 2000 (FSMA) is its primary legislation. The FSMA provides for a general prohibition against the provision of financial services without authorisation. Such authorisation is not usually granted unless the applicant is fit and proper.

◆ In June 2010, the Chancellor announced the government's intention to restructure the UK's financial regulatory framework and as part of this regulatory reform, the FSA will be replaced with two new successor regulatory bodies.

◆ The FSMA gives the FSA the four regulatory objectives. These objectives are market confidence, financial stability, the protection of consumers and the reduction of financial crime. It describes the general functions of the FSA as making rules under the FSMA, preparing and issuing codes under the FSMA, the giving of general guidance, and determining the general policy and principles by reference to which it performs its functions.

◆ The FSA has moved towards principles-based regulation with emphasis on principles and desirable outcomes where possible. The FSA's 11 principles for business are contained in the FSA Handbook and are fundamental obligations of all firms.

◆ The FSA uses a framework (ARROW II) to assess the risk that an authorised person poses to its regulatory objectives. The ARROW II process identifies risks to the FSA's statutory objectives and provides for risk-based supervision of the organisation on an ongoing basis.

◆ The Data Protection Act 1998 (DPA) protects the privacy rights and freedoms of individuals in the processing of personal data. Data controllers must adhere to eight data protection principles. Offences under the DPA are criminal; however, they do not carry prison sentences.

◆ Insider dealing occurs when an individual with inside information (price-sensitive information) uses this information in relation to securities (that are price-affected) in order to make a profit (or avoid a loss), thus gaining an advantage that would not be available to the general public. Insider dealing is a criminal offence under the Criminal Justice Act 1993.

◆ Market abuse involves behaviour in relation to investments which are trading (or have applied to trade) on a UK market. Market abuse is not a criminal offence and so conviction will not result in a jail sentence.

◆ The three main elements of the Retail Distribution Review (adviser charging, independent advice and professionalism) are intended to raise the standards investors can expect from all investment advisers. The new rules will come into effect on 31 December 2012.

◆ The standards set by international bodies such as the International Organization of Securities Commissions and the International Association of Insurance Supervisors have had an impact on the regulation of financial services business. Other bodies such as the Offshore Group of Insurance Supervisors also play a useful role for offshore financial services business providers.

Chapter ten
Money laundering

List of topics

Introduction

Money laundering
Money laundering occurs whenever there is an arrangement involving the proceeds of crime.

This chapter explains what is meant by **money laundering** and outlines the three stages of the traditional model of money laundering, placement, layering and integration. The harmful effects of money laundering that motivate various international bodies such as the FATF to cooperate are discussed, as are some of the more influential anti-money laundering/countering the financing of terrorism (AML/CFT) initiatives. The chapter outlines what a typical AML/CFT framework in an offshore centre may consist of, using the UK's framework as an example. The UK's substantive offences of money laundering (the concealing offence, the arranging offence and the acquisition offence) and the penalties involved are also explained. The offences of 'tipping off' and 'failure to report' are explained together with the penalties for these offences. Customer due diligence requirements and how these differ from those of the 'know your client' approach are discussed. Money laundering in offshore centres is discussed, as is the impact of the AML/CFT legislation on the offshore administrative environment. The chapter concludes with general 'red flags' which can assist a service provider to identify money laundering.

1. What is money laundering?

Money laundering involves the processing ('laundering') of criminal property (for example, by concealing, disguising or converting it) in order to give it the appearance of having arisen from a legitimate source.

Money laundering occurs whenever there is an arrangement involving the proceeds of crime (although, as explained in section 6 of this chapter, an offence will not necessarily be committed). What constitutes money laundering differs somewhat from jurisdiction to jurisdiction, depending on the laws that create the offences. The term 'money laundering' is slightly misleading as it implies that 'money' must be involved. In fact, the proceeds of crime involved could be in the form of any asset – for example, a property or a boat.

Profit from crime may arise as a result of many crimes including, but not limited to:

◆ organised crime;

◆ drug dealing;

◆ illegal arms trades;

◆ people trafficking;

◆ embezzlement;

◆ insider dealing;

◆ theft;

◆ tax evasion; and

◆ terrorist financing.

If the money laundering process is successful, the criminals can benefit and control the proceeds while avoiding their detection and confiscation.

2. The traditional model of money laundering

Historically, the money laundering process has been described as involving three main stages: placement, layering and integration.

1. **Placement** involves placing the proceeds of crime into the financial system. This could be achieved by depositing the proceeds of crime into a bank account.

2. **Layering** could involve using a complex system of transactions designed to hide the source and ownership of the funds. Trusts and companies located across jurisdictions could be used to achieve this.

3. **Integration** involves reintroducing the funds into the economy, so they appear to have originated from a legitimate source.

There are limitations in describing money laundering in terms of these three stages, as it is not necessarily the case that they will always be present. Money

Placement
A stage of the money laundering process which involves placing the proceeds of crime into the financial system (e.g. by depositing the proceeds of crime into a bank account).

Layering
A stage of the money laundering process which is designed to hide the source and ownership of criminal property (e.g. by using a complex system of transactions).

Integration
This is a stage of the money laundering process that involves reintroducing the criminal property into the economy, appearing to have originated from a legitimate source.

laundering instead can take a variety of forms ranging from very simple to very complex arrangements and it is therefore far more useful to be able to recognise the 'red flags' of money laundering, some of which are discussed later in this chapter.

Stop and think 10.1

Would the three stages described by the traditional model of money laundering be useful in assisting you to recognise money laundering where the proceeds of crime arose as a result of insider dealing (discussed in Chapter 9)?

3. The harmful effects of money laundering

The following is a non-exhaustive list of examples of the harmful and wide-ranging effects of money laundering on a country.

- The crimes that give rise to the proceeds that are laundered are extremely damaging to the victims and to society as a whole.

- Money laundering undermines democracy by allowing crime to be rewarded and allows organised criminals to expand their enterprise and become entrenched in society.

Corruption
Transparency International defines corruption as 'the misuse of entrusted power for private gain'. Public sector corruption involves, for example, the diversion of state funds for the benefit of politicians' own families.

- Money laundering rewards **corruption**. Corruption has a devastating effect on developing countries and seriously affects the quality of life and well-being of the citizens of those countries.

- Money laundering undermines the legitimate private sector. Organised criminals have access to substantial illegal funds enabling them to offer products at subsidised rates, thereby securing a competitive advantage over legitimate business.

- Money laundering makes tax collection more difficult, causing taxes to rise for those that pay and less resource to be available for healthcare or other social support required by people in need of these services.

- The integrity of the banking and financial services marketplace can be undermined if it does not (or is perceived not to) function within a framework of high legal, professional and ethical standards. Customers, financial intermediaries and regulatory authorities' perception of a jurisdiction will be adversely impacted. Legitimate business will not gravitate to jurisdictions that are perceived to be subject to the control and influence of organised crime and it will therefore be more difficult to attract foreign investment.

- Money laundering causes a risk to the soundness of banks and has been linked to the collapse of banks and other financial institutions. Where there is a concentration of criminal funds within an organisation, difficulties can arise if criminals suddenly withdraw their funds in order to avoid detection.

◆ When criminal funds are invested, the rate of the return which may be obtained is not necessarily the primary reason for investing in any particular jurisdiction or currency. Instead there may be more concern with keeping the funds undetected. This may lead to increased volatility of international capital flows and exchange rates due to unanticipated cross-border asset transfers and inexplicable changes in money demand affecting interest rates.

For service providers that become involved in money laundering, whether intentionally or not, there are significant consequences.

◆ The reputation of the organisation would be severely damaged. This damage could also have an effect on the reputation of other organisations in the jurisdiction, the jurisdiction itself, its regulators and any other person who has or was considering dealing with the institution.

◆ The regulatory risk for an organisation in a well-regulated organisation is likely to be great. A regulator could impose sanctions such as fines or restrictions (for example, on the firm's ability to take on new business) or require a report relating to the quality of the AML systems and controls within the business to be commissioned at the organisation's expense. Ultimately, a service provider could have its licence to operate within the jurisdiction revoked.

◆ The risk of criminal prosecution for money laundering exists at both the organisational and individual employee level.

◆ For the principal or key persons of the financial institution, the consequences could involve an assessment by the regulator of whether or not they are 'fit and proper' persons. This could lead to a variety of sanctions being imposed – for example, the individual may be prevented from obtaining further employment within a financial services business, or a public statement could be made.

◆ The risk financially in becoming involved in money laundering is great. In addition to the costs of complying with any remediation plan imposed by regulators, the organisation may be exposed to the risk of litigation.

Test yourself 10.1

Describe two of the harmful effects of money laundering.

4. Terrorist financing

The Terrorism Act 2000 describes terrorism as the use of or threat of action which:

◆ involves serious violence against a person;

◆ involves serious damage to property;

◆ endangers a person's life, other than that of the person committing the action;

◆ creates a serious risk to the health or safety of the public or a section of the public; or

◆ is designed seriously to interfere with or seriously to disrupt an electronic system.

The terrorist attacks on the World Trade Centre on 11 September 2001 have placed terrorism high on the international agenda and CFT measures are now often discussed synonymously with AML issues.

Terrorist financing differs from money laundering in fundamental ways. For example:

◆ the ultimate objective is to cause intimidation to a population;

◆ the funds used to finance terrorism do not necessarily arise from criminal conduct.

This can make it very difficult to identify. Although there are fundamental differences between money laundering and terrorist financing, they do have some features in common as those involved will usually still wish to conceal or disguise the ownership, movement and ultimate destination of the funds.

4.1 The UN Security Council Resolution 1373

The UN Security Council Resolution 1373 was adopted in September 2001. This imposed a requirement for participating countries to implement measures to combat terrorism. The measures are aimed at freezing the funds of terrorists, prohibiting the financing of terrorists, ensuring that offences are established to punish terrorism and to ensure that terrorists are not provided with a safe haven by participating countries.

4.2 International financial sanctions

The UK Implements UN Security Council Resolutions through the Terrorism (United Nations Measures) Orders 2006. Similar orders have been made in some offshore centres such as the Crown Dependencies.

4.3 The Terrorism Act 2000

The offences created by the Terrorism Act 2000 are aimed at criminalising:

◆ the receipt of funds for, or the provision of funds for, the purposes of terrorism;

◆ involvement in an arrangement that may involve an asset being made available for the purposes of terrorism.

Under the Terrorism Act 2000, it is an offence to fail to disclose a suspected offence of terrorism where there are reasonable grounds to know or suspect terrorism. There is also an offence which criminalises the disclosure of information to any person that is likely to prejudice any investigation. This is known as the 'tipping off' offence.

4.4 The FATF's 9 special recommendations

The FATF's special recommendations (discussed in section 5 of this chapter) set the international standard and cover areas such as the requirement to ratify and implement the United Nations (UN) instruments. The FATF recommendations require members to ratify and implement the 1999 UN International Convention for the suppression of the financing of terrorism and to implement the UN resolutions, particularly resolution 1373.

Test yourself 10.2

What is terrorist financing and how does it differ from money laundering?

5. International bodies and AML initiatives

There are compelling social and macro-economic reasons for governments to want to deter people from money laundering. However, there is little incentive for any jurisdiction to place itself at the forefront of AML regulation if the result may be to place its finance industry at a competitive disadvantage as funds simply flow to an alternative jurisdiction that has weaker AML controls. It is therefore recognised that a global approach is required to combat the problem.

The first international initiatives during the 1980s focussed on prevention of the laundering of funds derived solely from drug-trafficking activity. Since then, the focus has expanded significantly to include all serious crimes in some jurisdictions and all crimes in others.

The following are some of the more influential international bodies and AML initiatives.

5.1 The Financial Action Task Force (FATF) on Money Laundering

The FATF is an inter-governmental policy-making body which was established in July 1989 by the Group of Seven (G-7) summit in Paris in order to coordinate an international response to the problem of money laundering.

The FATF acts on the basis of a mandate, set by member jurisdictions at ministerial level. It currently comprises 36 member jurisdictions and two regional organisations, representing most major financial centres in all parts of the globe. There are also associate members and more than 20 international bodies and organisations that have observer status.

The FATF works to generate political will to bring about national legislative and regulatory reforms in the money laundering and terrorist financing areas. Since its establishment, the FATF has focussed on three main activities:

1. developing and setting standards and promoting policies, at both national and international levels, to combat money laundering and terrorist financing;

2. ensuring effective compliance with the standards; and

3. identifying money laundering and terrorist financing threats.

In 1990, the FATF drew up its 40 recommendations as an initiative to combat the misuse of financial systems by persons laundering drug money. These have since been revised and a further nine special recommendations have been created, aimed at combating the funding of terrorism.

FATF is recognised as the global standard setter on AML and CFT issues by the United Nations, the International Monetary Fund and the World Bank. The 49 recommendations set the international standards for combating money laundering and terrorist financing.

The FATF 40 recommendations set out that countries should take immediate steps to become party to and implement fully the Vienna Convention, the Palermo Convention and the 1999 United Nations International Convention for the Suppression of the Financing of Terrorism. Countries are also encouraged to ratify and implement other relevant international conventions, such as the 1990 Council of Europe Convention on Laundering, Search, Seizure and Confiscation of the Proceeds from Crime and the 2002 Inter-American Convention against Terrorism.

The FATF 40 recommendations require countries to criminalise money laundering on the basis of the Vienna Convention and the Palermo Convention. The requirements are that countries ensure that intent and knowledge to prove the offence is in line with the standards set out in the conventions, including the concept that the mental state for the money laundering offences may be inferred from objective factual circumstances. In addition, countries must adopt measures to enable their authorities to confiscate property laundered and proceeds from money laundering or predicate offences. The recommendations also cover areas such as politically exposed persons (PEPs), the use of legal persons and arrangements, measures to identify beneficial owners, record keeping, and international cooperation and exchange of information.

While there is no legal requirement for countries to follow the FATF's recommendations and it has no legal enforcement powers or official sanctioning powers, the FATF is a highly influential organisation, as was demonstrated by the results of its NCCT initiative.

5.2 The FATF's NCCT initiative

Non co-operating countries and territories (NCCT)
One of the FATF's AML/CFT initiatives.

One method that FATF employed in order to increase compliance with its recommendations was the '**non co-operating countries and territories (NCCTs)** initiative' of 2000. Many offshore centres were reviewed as a part of the process of identifying NCCTs.

The FATF identified 23 jurisdictions which had not implemented sufficient measures to meet the standards set by its recommendations and published the list of NCCTs. Peer pressure proved to be a very effective way of encouraging the countries on the list to implement the required standard. Each NCCT worked towards improving AML/CFT processes and, in 2006, the last country was removed from the list.

The NCCT initiative attracted criticism for being arbitrary and lacking a consistent methodology. Since 2007, the FATF has instead analysed and published a list of high-risk jurisdictions, and called upon members to consider the risks arising from the deficiencies associated with each jurisdiction. It has also called on members to apply countermeasures to protect the financial system from the money laundering and terrorist financing risks emanating from Iran and the Democratic People's Republic of Korea. This is a new process that is designed to achieve the same positive results as the NCCT programme, but in a different way. Continued non-compliance by a country for not meeting the standards can lead to these sanctions which are designed to encourage compliance and ultimately could lead to the termination of membership.

Making it work 10.1: The FATF's 40+9 recommendations in action

Offshore centres do not always attract desirable media coverage. They are often portrayed to be secretive tax havens where clients arrive with suitcases full of cash. There have been various BBC *Panorama* episodes where the presenter is located on a beach holding suitcases of cash while discussing offshore centres. In a BBC *Panorama* short documentary entitled 'How Tax Evasion Works', the presenter states that 'Critics say that tax havens such as Jersey, Guernsey, the Cayman Islands, the Isle of Man and Liechtenstein can help millionaires, tax cheats, dictators or terrorists to hide their money from the tax man or authorities'.

However, a review of the results of the ratings of compliance with the FATF's 40+9 recommendations applied to various jurisdictions following formal assessments reveals that offshore centres such as Jersey, Guernsey, Cyprus, Panama, the Cayman Islands and Malta were all rated as compliant or largely compliant with more of the recommendations than the UK. The Isle of Man was compliant or largely compliant with the same number of recommendations as the UK.

5.3 The Vienna Convention

The United Nations Convention against Illicit Traffic in Narcotic Drugs and Psychotropic Substances 1988 (also known as the Vienna Convention) came into force in 11 November 1990.

The aim of the Vienna Convention is to promote cooperation among the countries that are a party to it in order to assist them to address the international aspects of illicit traffic in narcotic drugs and psychotropic substances more effectively. Parties to the convention agree to take necessary measures to cooperate internationally (including legislative and administrative methods) in order to combat the trafficking of illegal drugs.

5.4 The Palermo Convention

The United Nations Convention against Transnational Organized Crime, 2000 (also known as the Palermo Convention) is the main international instrument in the fight against transnational organised crime. The Palermo Convention entered into force on 29 September 2003.

The Palermo Convention signifies the recognition by member countries of the seriousness of the problems posed by organised crime, as well as the need for international cooperation in order to tackle those problems. Countries that ratify this instrument commit themselves to taking a series of measures against transnational organised crime, including the creation of domestic criminal offences (participation in an organised criminal group, money laundering, corruption and obstruction of justice), the adoption of frameworks for extradition, mutual legal assistance and law enforcement cooperation; and the promotion of training and technical assistance.

5.5 The International Monetary Fund

The International Monetary Fund (IMF) came into formal existence in 1945 as a specialised agency of the United Nations when a number of countries came together to establish a framework for international economic cooperation after the Second World War. As of October 2011, the IMF has 187 member countries.

As explained earlier in this chapter, money laundering negatively affects economies and financial stability. This is of concern to the IMF as its fundamental mission is to help to ensure stability in the international system. The IMF provides technical assistance in the financial sector and exercises surveillance over members' economic systems. Unlike the FATF, the IMF does not seek to set AML/CFT standards; instead, it plays an important role in evaluating jurisdictional compliance with them.

5.6 The Group of International Finance Centre Supervisors (GIFCS)

The Offshore Group of Banking Supervisors was formed in October 1980 at the instigation of the Basel Committee on Banking Supervision as an association of the authorities concerned with the supervision of banks in offshore finance centres and the related financial services. The group changed its name to the Group of International Finance Centre Supervisors (GIFCS) in March 2011, in order to reflect better the wider scope of its activities.

Some jurisdictions such as Jersey, Guernsey, the Isle of Man and Gibraltar are not members of the FATF; however, they are members of the GIFCS which is an FATF observer. This means that members of the group have endorsed their commitments to the FATF recommendations.

5.7 The Council of Europe

As a prerequisite of membership of the European Union (EU), national governments must implement European Council (EC) AML directives. Member states were expected to implement the third European directive by December 2007. This replaced the first and second directives (agreed in June 1991 and December 2001) and is in line with the FATF recommendations.

5.8 The Wolfsberg Group

The Wolfsberg Group is an industry association of 11 global banks. The group worked with representatives from Transparency International to draft Anti-Money Laundering Principles for Private Banking ('the Wolfsberg Principles') which were published in October 2000 and revised in May 2002. The group aims to develop financial services industry standards for knowing your customer and AML/CFT policies, and acts as a mechanism for the banking industry to cooperate in order to achieve this.

The Wolfsberg principles cover:

◆   client acceptance: general guidelines;
◆   client acceptance: situations requiring additional diligence/attention;
◆   updating client files;
◆   practices when identifying unusual or suspicious activities;
◆   monitoring;
◆   control responsibilities;
◆   reporting;
◆   education, training and information;
◆   record retention requirements;
◆   exceptions and deviations; and
◆   anti-money laundering organisation.

In 2002, the group also published a statement on the financing of terrorism.

5.9 The Basel Committee on Banking Supervision

The Basel Committee on Banking Supervision is made up of a representative from each central bank and a representative from the body with formal responsibility for the prudential supervision of banking business in each country. The Committee cannot impose legally binding standards; however, it has formulated broad supervisory standards and guidelines known as the Basel Principles which encourage banks to implement measures to prevent money laundering.

The Committee published a paper entitled 'The Prevention of Criminal Use of the Banking System for the Purpose of Money Laundering' in 1988. The paper is a statement of principles to which financial institutions should be expected to adhere and is intended to outline some basic policies and procedures that a bank's management should ensure are in place within their institutions with a view to assisting in the suppression of money laundering through the banking system. The paper covers areas such as:

◆ customer identification;

◆ compliance with laws;

◆ cooperation with law enforcement authorities; and

◆ the requirements for banks to formally adopt policies consistent with the principles contained within the statement (e.g. provision of training, implement procedures for customer identification, retention of records of transactions, etc.).

In addition, the Basel Committee issued a paper entitled 'Customer due diligence for banks' in October 2001. Within this paper, the committee states that it strongly supports the adoption and implementation of the FATF recommendations. The Committee's approach to 'know your customer' (KYC) was from a wider perspective than merely AML. The paper addresses four essential elements of KYC standards:

1. customer acceptance policy;

2. customer identification issues (including issues arising from trust and corporate vehicles, introduced business, politically exposed persons (PEPs) and non-face-to-face customers);

3. ongoing monitoring of accounts and transactions; and

4. risk management.

In February 2003, the committee published a 'General guide to account opening and customer identification'. This is a guide to good practice and is based on the 2001 paper 'Customer due diligence for banks'.

In October 2004, the committee published a paper entitled 'Consolidated KYC Risk Management' on establishing KYC processes on a group-wide basis.

5.10 The United Nations Office on Drugs and Crime

The United Nations Office on Drugs and Crime (UNODC) was set up by the United Nations in 1997 to implement the United Nations International Drug Control Program and its Crime Prevention and Criminal Justice Program. The overall aims of the UNODC are to assist UN member states in the struggle against illicit drugs, crime and terrorism. It does this through:

◆ research and analytical work;

◆ helping countries to implement treaties, draft domestic legislation; and

◆ providing other assistance such as the training of judicial officials.

The UNODC has issued model legislation for both common law and civil law legal systems to assist countries to set up legislation that meets the standards set by FATF and other international initiatives.

Test yourself 10.3

a) Why is a global approach crucial in the fight against money laundering and terrorism?

b) Outline the roles of two of the more influential international bodies that have encouraged international cooperation.

6. AML legislation

Legislation that criminalises the handling of proceeds of crime is designed to prevent criminal funds from entering the financial system and to ensure that, where they do, they can be detected and confiscated.

All national AML frameworks have developed as a result of the influence of international bodies and international initiatives such as those of the FATF and the EU. As a result, the principles and the wording used within AML legislation are often similar.

It is therefore possible to gain an understanding of the AML frameworks in many offshore jurisdictions by using the UK framework as many offshore jurisdictions have implemented similar frameworks. AML frameworks typically comprise of primary legislation, secondary legislation and guidance notes.

6.1 Primary legislation

The primary legislation contains the criminal offences of money laundering. In the UK, the primary legislation is the Proceeds of Crime Act 2002 (PoCA).

The PoCA creates three substantive offences of money laundering. These include:

◆ the concealing offence;
◆ the arranging offence; and
◆ the acquisition, use or possession offence.

The concealing offence
Article 327 sets out that a person commits an offence if they:

a) conceal criminal property;

b) disguise criminal property;

c) convert criminal property;

d) transfer criminal property; or

e) remove the criminal property from England and Wales or from Scotland or Northern Ireland.

Under Article 327, concealing or disguising 'criminal property' includes concealing or disguising its nature, source, location, disposition, movement or ownership or any rights with respect to it.

The PoCA sets out that property is 'criminal property' if:

1. It constitutes a benefit from criminal conduct; *and*
2. the alleged offender *knows or suspects* that the property is as a result of criminal conduct.

Money laundering as an activity can therefore occur without an offence being committed – for example, the trustee who deals with criminal property is engaged in the activity of money laundering; however, an offence will not be committed unless the trustee knows or suspects that the property is as a result of criminal conduct.

The arranging offence
Article 328 of the PoCA sets out that a person commits an offence if they enter into an arrangement which they know or suspect involves the proceeds of crime. This is a very widely drafted offence and would capture the provision of professional services, such as acting as trustee.

The acquisition, use or possession offence
Under Article 329 of PoCA, an offence is committed where a person acquires, uses or has possession of criminal property.

Penalties
The maximum penalty for all of the substantive offences of money laundering in the UK is 14 years' imprisonment or a fine, or both.

Defences
A person does not commit an offence under Article 327, 328 or 329 if they make an authorised disclosure (i.e. disclosure to a nominated officer) *before* they do the act and they have the appropriate consent (for example, the consent of the **Serious Organised Crime Agency** (**SOCA**)) to do the act. The nominated officer is often known as a Money Laundering Reporting Officer (MLRO).

Serious Organised Crime Agency (SOCA)
The FIU in the UK.

The failure to report offence
The primary legislation in many jurisdictions imposes a direct obligation on employees in financial services business to make a suspicious activity report (SAR) if they suspect that money laundering has taken place.

Article 330 of the PoCA contains the 'failure to disclose' offence for those in the regulated sector. It sets out that a person commits an offence if three conditions are satisfied.

1. They know or suspect or have reasonable grounds for knowing or suspecting that another person is engaged in money laundering.

2. The information on which their knowledge or suspicion (or reasonable grounds for knowledge or suspicion) is based came to them in the course of a business.

3. They do not make the required disclosure as soon as practicable after the information or other matter comes to them.

Many jurisdictions now apply the 'objective test' to the substantive money laundering offences. This means that actual knowledge or suspicion that a person is dealing with the proceeds of crime is not required. Instead, the test is whether a reasonable person would have formed a suspicion of money laundering. This differs from the more historic subjective test where actual knowledge or suspicion was required in order to commit the offence of money laundering.

The maximum penalty for failure to disclose is five years' imprisonment, or a fine, or both.

Suspicious activity reports

The report made to the nominated officer is known as a suspicious activity report (SAR). SARs are sometimes referred to as suspicious transaction reports (STRs) although the term SARs is now more widely used as this reflects the fact that a transaction need not necessarily take place for money laundering to be present.

A SAR includes details of the persons involved and the reasons for the suspicion. The nominated officer analyses the report and, taking all of the circumstances into consideration, decides whether or not in their opinion, the activity does give rise to a suspicion of money laundering. If they decide that it does, they make an external report to the **Financial Intelligence Unit (FIU)**. In the UK, the FIU is SOCA, who may then give consent to proceed with a transaction, thus providing a defence to the offence of money laundering as explained above.

Financial Intelligence Unit (FIU)
Used to describe the authority in a jurisdiction which has responsibility for receiving and dealing with suspicious activity reports from financial institutions.

The tipping off offence

Under Article 333, a person who knows or suspects that a suspicious activity report has been made commits an offence if they disclose to another person information which is likely to prejudice any investigation which might be conducted.

The PoCA contains a defence to the offence of tipping off where a person did not know or suspect that the disclosure was likely to be prejudicial.

The maximum penalty for 'tipping off' is five years' imprisonment, or a fine, or both.

6.2 Secondary legislation

The secondary legislation in the UK is in the form of the Money Laundering Regulations 2007 which implements the EU third European Directive. Secondary legislation is often referred to as 'regulations' or 'orders' and usually contains the procedural requirements that financial institutions are required to comply with. The Money Laundering Regulations 2007 impose a number of requirements on 'relevant persons'. Relevant persons consist of financial institutions, legal professionals and trust company service providers, among other institutions.

The Money Laundering Regulations 2007 set out requirements in relation to:

◆   customer due diligence;

◆   record keeping (a person must keep records evidencing the customer identity documents obtained for five years after the business relationship ends to enable a relevant person to demonstrate compliance with the legislation);

◆   policies and procedures; and

◆   training.

The policies and procedures that a relevant person must establish and maintain must be *appropriate* and *risk-sensitive* policies and procedures relating to:

◆   customer due diligence measures (including a requirement to identify and verify a customer's identity and which identify whether the customer is a PEP);

◆   ongoing monitoring (providing for identification and scrutiny of unusual transactions or activity that may indicate money laundering);

◆   reporting knowledge or suspicion that a person is engaged in money laundering or terrorist financing (including a requirement to appoint an MLRO);

◆   record keeping;

◆   internal control;

◆   risk assessment and management; and

◆   the monitoring and management of compliance with and internal communication of such policies and procedures.

Case law 10.1: The Attorney General v. Caversham Fiduciary Services Limited and Caversham Trustees Limited and Nicholas Bell (Caversham) 2006 JLR61

In 2002, Caversham, a Jersey trust company, was approached by a solicitor who explained that an attorney who acted for a third party, Mr Lee, wished to set up a trust to hold the proceeds from the sale of a sauna business.

Caversham created the trust (with the attorney as the sole beneficiary) and received documentation in relation to the identity of the attorney, but not the ultimate client. Upon receipt of the trust fund (£850,000) from the solicitor's account, Caversham were asked (and agreed to) pay the funds to four entitles which were not connected to the trust.

An order made pursuant to the primary legislation in Jersey required procedures to be 'maintained' by persons carrying on financial services business, for the purpose of forestalling and preventing money laundering. The procedures were to include measures to establish the identity of the person on whose behalf an applicant for business acted.

Caversham and Nicholas Bell (a principal person) were charged and convicted with forming a business relationship without 'maintaining' procedures in relation to identification.

On appeal, it was argued that an offence could only be committed by a systemic failure to 'maintain' the procedures required under the law and not by a single instance of failure. The Attorney General submitted that 'maintain' means 'to keep up' in the same way that, in common usage, a boxer who drops his gloves and allows a knockout blow is said to have failed to maintain his guard.

The appeals were dismissed and the convictions upheld in 2006.

The training that a relevant person must provide includes taking appropriate measures so that all relevant employees are made aware of the law relating to money laundering and terrorist financing, and regularly given training in how to recognise and deal with transactions and activities that may be related to money laundering or terrorist financing.

6.3 Industry guidance

In the UK, the Senior Management Systems and Controls Sourcebook (SYSC) contains high-level guidance. In addition, however, firms are expected to follow the guidance issued by the Joint Money Laundering Steering Group (JMLSG).

The JMLSG is made up of the leading UK trade associations in the finance industry. It has no regulatory function. Failure to follow the guidance is not considered to be a breach of the regulations or the FSA Handbook.

The regulatory authorities in many jurisdictions have issued guidance to assist financial institutions to interpret the regulations and understand their obligations under the primary and secondary legislation. The words 'guidance' could imply that financial institutions need not follow it; however, in well-regulated jurisdictions, a failure to follow the guidance is considered a serious matter as regulations often state that in deciding whether an offence has been committed, the court must consider whether the defendant followed any relevant guidance approved by an appropriate body.

Test yourself 10.4

Outline the content of a typical AML framework for an offshore jurisdiction.

7. Know your customer (KYC) and customer due diligence (CDD)

7.1 Know your customer (KYC)

When AML/CFT legislation and guidance began to develop, many jurisdictions implemented simple identification requirements. The term KYC became associated with the need for financial institutions to obtain a copy of their client's passports and two utility bills. This tick-box approach was not particularly helpful to the AML cause. While identifying the client plays an important part in the prevention and detection of money laundering, these measures alone are inadequate.

7.2 Customer due diligence (CDD)

Today, the requirements are referred to as customer due diligence (CDD), an approach that requires not only the collection of information from financial institutions but the forming of a customer due diligence profile which enables a financial institution to understand what to expect from the business relationship and to facilitate ongoing monitoring (scrutinising of transactions). Understanding expectations will enable a financial institution to recognise unusual or suspicious activity and to take any necessary action. This may involve asking further questions in order to become comfortable with the transaction or may involve making a suspicious activity report.

The Money Laundering Regulations 2007 set out that financial institutions must maintain procedures in relation to customer due diligence measures that include a requirement to:

◆ identify the customer;
◆ verify the customer's identity on the basis of documents or information obtained from a reliable independent source; and
◆ obtain relationship information at the outset of the relationship.

The extent of information and verification undertaken may be determined in accordance with a risk-based approach, which will be discussed later in this chapter. Documents such as a copy of the client's passport (which has been certified by an independent and 'suitable certifier', e.g. a professional such as a lawyer) or other government-issued documents and original (or certified copies) utility bills are often collected during this process.

Relationship information includes information such as:

◆ the source of wealth;
◆ the source of funds;
◆ the purpose and nature of the business relationship (rationale); and
◆ the expected activity of the client including the volume and value of transactions.

Detailed ways in which a financial institution can meet the requirements of the legislation are set out in the industry guidance.

Risk-based approach

International standards set by the FATF and other international bodies advocate a risk-based approach to CDD. This involves the financial institution undertaking a risk assessment of its clients and then deciding the appropriate level of CDD information and verification to collect the appropriate level of transaction monitoring and reviewing to apply to the customer relationships on an ongoing basis. A risk-based approach allows a financial institution to focus resources on areas where the risk of money laundering or terrorist financing is higher and therefore allows a proportionate and cost-effective approach to managing the risk.

Relationships involving politically exposed persons (individuals who are or have been entrusted with prominent public function and their families), for example, are relationships that present a higher risk of money laundering. For these individuals, enhanced due diligence should be undertaken on a risk-sensitive basis.

Enhanced due diligence (EDD) involves:

- obtaining further CDD information;
- taking additional steps to verify the CDD information;
- requiring higher levels of management approval for higher-risk new customers; and
- requiring more frequent reviews of the relationship.

8. Money laundering in offshore centres

The vulnerability to money laundering in any jurisdiction should, whether onshore or offshore, be considered in light of the effectiveness of the laws, the political will and resource available to enforce them. As discussed in section 6, AML/CFT frameworks in many offshore centres are comparable to those of the onshore jurisdictions.

That said, the features of offshore centres can prove useful to money laundering, as the following sets out.

8.1 Secrecy laws and confidentiality provisions

Some offshore jurisdictions are subject to secrecy laws or confidentiality provisions and this can make it difficult to achieve cross-border exchange of information for the purposes of preventing or detecting money laundering.

By way of an example, Luxembourg's financial institutions are subject to professional secrecy laws. The FATF's mutual evaluation report (2009) explained how the laws are lifted to certain authorities but not their Financial Intelligence Unit (FIU), the unit that receives suspicious activity reports. STRs are analysed very thoroughly before reporting to the FIU, for fear of prosecution for violating professional secrecy, the penalty for which is higher than the penalty for failing to file an STR. Laws such as these will inevitably hinder transparency as they may prevent information about suspicions from reaching the FIU and the laws may be invoked against an FIU, preventing them from investigating reports received. If the FIU cannot access this information, it cannot share it with other jurisdictions.

8.2 Asset protection legislation

Offshore centres often have legislation which ensures that the assets within a structure can only be attacked by action in the local courts. This makes it considerably more costly and complex for authorities outside of the jurisdiction to make such an attack.

8.3 Products and services

Many products available onshore and offshore can be used to launder money, including insurance products, bank accounts and investment schemes. The products that considerably increase the vulnerability of offshore centres to money laundering include:

◆   the extensive use of legal persons (i.e. those that are incorporated by law) including companies, foundations and the Liechtenstein Anstalt; and

◆   the extensive use of legal arrangements (i.e. trusts).

Both legal persons and arrangements are used for legitimate business purposes; however, their features present significant opportunities for those who wish to distance themselves from the proceeds of their crimes and to retain the benefit of their crimes at the same time. Some of the vulnerabilities with these types of products and related services are discussed below.

Legal persons
Legal persons contract and transact business in their own name. The use of directors provided by a service provider or the use of corporate directors (usually a company owned by the service provider) means that transactions are undertaken on behalf of the company by these directors, thus negating the need for the client to be associated with the transaction.

The extent of information available from the Companies Registry varies significantly from one jurisdiction to another. Some, for example, require information on beneficial ownership at the time of incorporation but do not impose any obligation to update the Registry where this changes.

While it is often a requirement to inform the authorities of the identity of the shareholders (legal owners), this information is not useful in establishing beneficial ownership as the use of nominee shareholders is routinely provided by trust and company service providers in offshore centres. With the use of nominee shareholders, a declaration is signed by the service provider admitting and declaring that they hold the shares as nominee for the customer absolutely and that they will do with the shares as they are instructed to do.

A company must usually disclose the address of its registered office to the Companies Registry. This address is, however, usually that of a service provider and the company's physical presence (if it has one) is not necessarily located there.

Bearer shares are a feature of some companies that renders any CDD undertaken useless as soon as the shares change hands.

The authorities in a well-regulated jurisdiction should have access to the files of the service provider; however, they may still have difficulty identifying the 'human face' behind a company, particularly if is owned by another company, registered in another jurisdiction or if the shares are owned by a legal arrangement or have been issued in bearer form.

Legal arrangements

Most jurisdictions do not require trusts to be registered in the same way as companies and therefore the existence of a trust is not a matter of public record. The benefit of any register would only be as valuable as the information that is contained in the trust deed and this can be minimal.

In law, a trust is recognised without any written documentation (although it is unlikely that a regulated trust company in an AML-aware jurisdiction would operate in this manner).

In the past, 'dummy settlors' have been named in trust documentation, disguising the settlor. While this practice is no longer prevalent in well-regulated jurisdictions, it is still acceptable for an instrument referred to as a Declaration of Trust which does not contain the name of the settlor to document the terms of the trust.

Where a settlor's details are recorded on the trust deed, only the first provider of funds is recorded on the documentation. However, trusts are flexible in nature and would usually allow further funds to be added.

A person's ability to benefit can be hidden. It is not uncommon to find that trust documentation has been prepared with only a well-known charity as the named beneficiary. Again, this is an outdated practice.

Beneficiaries can be included in a 'class' of beneficiaries that does not make it obvious who in fact will receive benefit or they can be appointed at a later date. All of these features could present significant opportunity for money launderers and service providers should be aware of the vulnerabilities.

Bearer shares
Shares which are considered to be owned by 'the bearer', i.e. whoever has them in their possession. Cash is an example of a bearer instrument.

Test yourself 10.5

How could the features of a company be useful to a person who intends to launder the proceeds of crime?

9. Recognising money laundering

The best way to ensure that unusual or suspicious activity is identified is to understand the purpose of each business relationship and what can be expected from it.

There are, however, some general 'red flags' that could indicate money laundering. Of course the presence of one red flag alone may not necessarily mean that money laundering has occurred or is occurring; however, its presence should be understood. The following are examples.

- The receipt of *unusually* large cash deposits.
- The receipt of funds followed by an immediate request for these to be paid elsewhere.
- The use of multiple transfer requests where a single payment could have been sent. This could indicate an intention to avoid mandatory reporting limits that exist in some jurisdictions. Similarly, the receipt of multiple receipts for no apparent reason could indicate money laundering.
- A reluctance to receive payments directly.
- Requests for third-party receipts or payments without sufficient explanation – particularly where it is known to you that the funds will eventually reach your client.
- Use of multiple bank accounts or corporate entities that do not appear to serve a purpose. These can complicate a structure unnecessarily and could be useful in the layering process.
- The use of dummy settlors.
- The use of 'blind trusts'. There are legitimate uses for these; however, the reason for their use should be understood and be reasonable.
- A reluctance to provide usual due diligence information and a client who is reluctant for you to have direct contact with them.
- A client whose internet profile has adverse public information involving financial or other relevant crime.
- A lack of commercial rationale for the structure.
- A lack of legal or tax advice where the structure appears to be very complex and involving multiple entities or jurisdictions.
- The matching of payment requests to credits received on the same or previous day with no reasonable explanation.
- The use of previously dormant accounts.
- Unexpected early repayment of loans where the customer's means to do so is not apparent.
- The use of safe deposit boxes without reasonable cause.
- Dealings with parties located in known drug-trafficking areas or countries associated with known terrorist organisations.
- The purchase of insurance products together with subsequent early surrender or cancellation with no concern over surrender values.

◆ A lack of concern on the behalf of the client over the cost of transactions and no interest in minimising cost.

◆ A lack of a desire to receive reports on the performance of their investments or bank account balances.

Test yourself 10.6

Identify six 'red flags' that indicate that a customer may be using a bank account as a part of the money laundering process.

10. The impact of AML/CFT legislation on the administration environment in offshore centres

AML/CFT legislation has had a significant impact on the administrative environment in offshore centres. In general one can expect:

◆ to operate in an ever-increasingly regulated environment;

◆ to have to maintain numerous policies and procedures including those surrounding the customer due diligence process both at the acceptance of new business stage and on an ongoing basis;

◆ an increased standard of documentation and record keeping required in order to demonstrate compliance with the AML/CFT requirements;

◆ to receive AML training on at least an annual basis;

◆ to work in an organisation which has an adequately staffed compliance department including a Money Laundering Reporting Officer whose role it is to receive and deal with SARs and in some jurisdictions, a Money Laundering Compliance Officer whose role it is to monitor compliance specifically with the money laundering regulations of the jurisdiction;

◆ some resistance from historic client relationships who do not understand why a service provider with whom there is a long-standing relationship is suddenly insisting on receiving a lot of information. There may also be resistance where there are increased costs arising from the work involved in bringing the client files up to today's standards;

◆ an increased desire to obtain new business via trusted intermediaries and introducers;

◆ a requirement to undertake regular reviews of client entities (sometimes referred to as periodic or annual reviews) designed in part to facilitate transaction monitoring and to ensure that the customer due diligence documentation on file is still up to date and appropriate;

◆ a reluctance to accept cash payments into the structure and a reluctance to make cash distributions to beneficiaries or shareholders;

◆ a reluctance to make payments to or receive funds from third parties who have not been subject to the customer due diligence process;

◆ an increased awareness and use of open-source public information to monitor for adverse information in respect of customers.

Chapter summary

◆ Money laundering has wide-ranging harmful effects on society and on the macro-economy.

◆ Terrorism involves a threat of harm to a population. Its objectives differ from money laundering and the source of funds is not necessarily illegal.

◆ The FATF sets the international standards for AML/CFT through their 40+9 recommendations although there are various other influential bodies that help to facilitate a global approach to money laundering.

◆ AML frameworks in offshore centres are often similar to those in the UK due to the influence of international initiatives.

◆ The UK AML framework consists of primary legislation, secondary legislation and industry guidance. The primary legislation creates the principal offence of money laundering.

◆ The AML/CFT legislation creates obligations for financial institutions such as the requirement to report knowledge or suspicion of money laundering to SOCA, the requirement to maintain AML procedures such as CDD and record keeping.

◆ Offshore centres can be particularly vulnerable to money laundering due to the products that are widely available and due to the features of offshore centres.

◆ Money laundering can be recognised by 'red flags' and their presence in any business relationship should be understood.

◆ AML legislation has significantly changed the offshore administration environment.

Glossary

Anti-avoidance legislation Legislation that has been introduced in order to minimise the opportunities to minimise taxation via the use of offshore centres, particularly where the transaction has no purpose other than the minimisation of taxation.

Arising basis of taxation Under the arising basis of taxation, a person will pay UK tax on all of their income as it arises and on the gains as they accrue, wherever that income and those gains are in the world.

Bearer shares Shares which are considered to be owned by 'the bearer', i.e. whoever has them in their possession. Cash is an example of a bearer instrument.

Capacity A party to a contract must have legal capacity (the power legally to enter into it) for it to be enforceable. Vulnerable people such as children do not have capacity.

Chargeable asset An asset that may be subject to capital gains tax when it is disposed of (i.e. sold or given away).

Chargeable gain A gain made on the same of an asset that is liable to capital gains tax.

Common law A system of law under which the judges are guided by previous decisions of the courts under the doctrine of judicial precedent.

Consideration Consideration must be given by both parties to a contract and is defined as 'some right, interest, profit or benefit accruing to one party, or some forbearance, detriment, loss or responsibility given, suffered or undertaken by the other' (Currie v. Misa).

Corruption Transparency International defines corruption as 'the misuse of entrusted power for private gain'. Public sector corruption involves, for example, the diversion of state funds for the benefit of politicians' own families.

Data controller An organisation that processes personal data.

Deemed domiciled A person becomes deemed domiciled for IHT purposes if they have been present in the UK for any part of the last 17 out of 20 years including the tax year in question.

Direct taxes Taxes on income (e.g. income tax).

Doctrine of judicial precedent Under the doctrine of judicial precedent, the judge is bound to follow decisions that have been reached in earlier court cases.

Earned income Income that is earned – for example, salary or bonuses from employment or income from a trade or profession or from a pension.

Entities Used to describe both legal persons (such as companies) and legal arrangements (such as trusts).

Equity A system of law administered by the Court of Chancery that developed alongside the common law where justice could not be done.

Exchange control regulations Regulations or other controls that are imposed by the governments of some countries that fear or are experiencing scarcity of foreign currency (and often, precious metals). Such controls may limit or ban the amount of foreign or local currency that can be traded or purchased, or may involve controls which restrict residents from removing currency out of the jurisdiction.

Excluded property trust Excluded property trusts are those created by non-UK-domiciled individuals (who have not yet been deemed domiciled in the UK) with non-UK situs assets. Such trusts receive favourable IHT treatment.

Fiduciary relationship A relationship founded on trust. A person with a fiduciary duty has a duty to act in the best interests of another person.

Financial Intelligence Unit (FIU) Used to describe the authority in a jurisdiction which has responsibility for receiving and dealing with suspicious activity reports from financial institutions.

Financial services business Used to describe the carrying on of investment business, trust company business, general insurance mediation business, money services business or funds services business.

Fiscal policies Policies that relate to the public revenues (i.e. income from taxation).

Forced heirship In some countries, the laws require the assets held in a person's estate to pass to stated heirs (usually the person's spouse and children). This is known as forced heirship and such heirs are known as 'forced heirs' (or sometimes 'fixed heirs').

Gift with reservation A gift whereby the donor retains an interest in the asset (this could involve retaining a benefit or control of the asset).

Indirect taxes Taxes on expenditure (e.g. VAT).

Injunction A judicial order that restrains a person from doing something or orders someone do to something.

Inside information Information which relates to particular securities, is specific or precise, has not been made public and if it were made public, would be likely to have a significant effect on the price of any securities.

Insider dealing Insider dealing occurs when an individual with inside information (price-sensitive information) uses this information in relation to securities (that are price-affected) in order to make a profit (or avoid a loss), thus gaining an advantage that would not be available to the general public.

Integration This is a stage of the money laundering process that involves reintroducing the criminal property into the economy, appearing to have originated from a legitimate source.

Invitation to treat An invitation to another person to make an offer.

Jurisdiction A territory over which authority is exercised by laws which are under the control of a system of courts different to that of its neighbouring areas.

Layering A stage of the money laundering process which is designed to hide the source and ownership of criminal property (e.g. by using a complex system of transactions).

Legal arrangements Legal arrangements include fiduciary arrangements such as trusts.

Legal persons Those persons that are incorporated by law (e.g. companies).

Mareva injunction An order of the court which prevents a defendant to an action from disposing of the assets or transferring them from the jurisdiction.

Market abuse Behaviour in relation to investments which are trading (or have applied to trade) on a UK market.

Money laundering Money laundering occurs whenever there is an arrangement involving the proceeds of crime.

Non co-operating countries and territories (NCCT) One of the FATF's AML/CFT initiatives.

Obiter dicta The *obiter dicta* of a case are words that are said 'by the way' and do not form a part of the *ratio decidendi*.

Offshore centre A jurisdiction which seeks to create a competitive advantage through its laws and which provides financial services primarily to non-residents.

Person Used to refer to both natural persons such as individuals and legal persons (i.e. those that are created by law) such as companies.

Personal data Data that relates to a living individual (the data subject) who can be identified from that data.

Placement A stage of the money laundering process which involves placing the proceeds of crime into the financial system (e.g. by depositing the proceeds of crime into a bank account).

Principal persons Those individuals who control an organisation by way of directorships or shareholdings.

Quantum meruit This term means 'as much as he deserved'.

Ratio decidendi The *ratio decidendi* of a case is any rule of law or legal principle that is treated by the judge as necessary for the basis of the decision made.

Registered office The address of a company which has been notified to the authorities (as required by law) as the address to which legal notices can be sent.

Remittance basis of taxation Individuals who are non domiciled in the UK (or those who are not ordinarily resident in the UK) pay UK tax only on the amount of their foreign income and gains that they remit to the UK.

Rescission The revocation or cancellation of a contract. The effect is to bring the parties to the contract back to the position that they were in before the contract was effected.

Revocation An offer may terminated by revocation. This means that the offeror cancels the offer and it is not longer open for acceptance.

Serious Organised Crime Agency (SOCA) The FIU in the UK.

Service provider Organisations or individuals who provide financial services business offshore may simply be referred to as service providers.

Shadow director One who has not been formally appointed but who is deemed in law to be a director due to the function that they are fulfilling.

Source of funds Activities which generate funds for a relationship.

Source of wealth Activities which have generated the total net worth of a person.

Specific performance An equitable remedy that a court may make which orders the parties to the contract to fulfil their obligations under it.

Stare decisis A Latin term for 'let the decision stand'.

Structure Used to describe a group of trusts and companies that are connected by their ownership or their assets and are aimed at meeting the needs of a particular client or group of clients.

Tipping off This refers to the committing of an offence under Article 333 of the PoCA.

Transfer price The price that is agreed between two connected parties for the sale of goods or services.

Unearned income Unearned income includes income that is received from sources other than from employment (or a trade or profession).

Wasting asset An asset that has a limited life and therefore decreases in value over time, e.g. a car or a factory machine.

Directory of web resources

Basel Committee on Banking Supervision
www.bis.org/bcbs

British and Irish Legal Information Institute (BAILII)
www.bailii.org

British Virgin Islands Financial Services Commission
www.bvifsc.vg

The Cheque and Credit Clearing Company Limited
www.chequeandcredit.co.uk

The Financial Action Task Force (FATF)
www.fatf-gafi.org

The Group of International Finance Centre Supervisors
www.ogbs.net

Guernsey Financial Services Commission
www.gfsc.gg

HM Revenue & Customs
www.hmrc.gov.uk

International Association of Insurance Supervisors (IAIS)
www.iaisweb.org

International Monetary Fund (IMF)
www.imf.org

International Organization of Securities Commissions (IOSCO)
www.iosco.org

Jersey Finance Limited
www.jerseyfinance.je/About-Jersey/International-Finance-Centre

Jersey Financial Services Commission
www.jerseyfsc.org

Jersey Legal Information Board
www.jerseylaw.je

The Judicial Committee of the Privy Council
www.jcpc.gov.uk

The National Archives
www.legislation.gov.uk

Organisation for Economic Co-operation and Development (OECD)
www.oecd.org

The Payments Council
www.paymentscouncil.org.uk

The UK Payments Administration Limited
www.ukpayments.org.uk

Index